THE SAVIOUR
OF THE WORLD

THE SAVIOUR OF THE WORLD

BENJAMIN B. WARFIELD

THE BANNER OF TRUTH TRUST

THE BANNER OF TRUTH TRUST
3 Murrayfield Road, Edinburgh EH12 6EL
P.O. Box 621, Carlisle, Pennsylvania 17013, U.S.A.

*

First published 1916
First reprint by the Banner of Truth Trust 1991
ISBN 0 85151 593 2

*

Printed in Great Britain by Offset Lithography by
the Alden Press, Oxford.

To

The Senate

and

The Faculty of Theology

of the

University of Utrecht

in acknowledgment of

the Honorary Degree of Doctor of Theology

4 December, 1913

CONTENTS

CHAPTER I

CONTENTS

CHAPTER VII

CHAPTER VIII

CHAPTER IX

THE PRODIGAL SON

LUKE xv. 11–32 :—And he said, A certain man had two sons : and the younger of them said to his father, Father, give me the portion of thy substance that falleth to me. And he divided unto them his living. And not many days after the younger son gathered all together, and took his journey into a far country ; and there he wasted his substance with riotous living. And when he had spent all, there arose a mighty famine in that country ; and he began to be in want. And he went and joined himself to one of the citizens of that country ; and he sent him into his fields to feed swine. And he would fain have been filled with the husks that the swine did eat : and no man gave unto him. But when he came to himself he said, How many hired servants of my father's have bread enough and to spare, and I perish here with hunger ! I will arise and go to my father, and will say unto him, Father, I have sinned against heaven, and in thy sight: I am no more worthy to be called thy son : make me as one of thy hired servants. And he arose, and came to his father. But while he was yet afar off, his father saw him, and was moved with compassion, and ran, and fell on his neck, and kissed him. And the son said unto him, Father, I have sinned against heaven, and in thy sight : I am no more worthy to be called thy son. But the father said to his servants, Bring forth quickly the best robe, and put it on him ; and put a ring on his hand, and shoes on his feet : and bring the fatted calf, and kill it, and let us eat, and make merry : for this my son was dead, and is alive again ; he was lost, and is found. And they began to be merry. Now his elder son was in the field : and as he came and drew nigh to the house, he heard music and dancing. And he called to him one of the servants, and inquired what these things might be. And he said unto him, Thy brother is come ; and thy father hath killed the fatted calf, because he hath received him safe and sound. But he was angry, and would not go in : and his father came out, and intreated him. But he answered and said to his father, Lo, these many years do I serve thee, and I never transgressed a commandment of thine : and yet thou never gavest me a kid, that I might make merry with my friends : but when this thy son came, which hath devoured thy living with harlots, thou killedst for him the fatted calf. And he said unto him, Son, thou art ever with me, and all that is mine is thine. But it was meet to make merry and be glad : for this thy brother was dead, and is alive again ; and was lost, and is found.

THE PRODIGAL SON

I WISH to speak to you to-day of the parable of the prodigal son, or, as it is becoming very common to call it, perhaps with greater exactness, the parable of the lost son. I shall not read it to you again. It has already been read in the lesson for the day. And in any event it is too familiar to require that you should be reminded even of the minuter details of the narrative. Probably no passage of the Scriptures is more widely known or more universally admired. The conversation and literature of devotion are full of allusions to it. And in the conversation and literature of the world it has far from an unhonoured place.

It owes the high appreciation it has won, no doubt, in large part to the exquisiteness of its literary form. From this point of view it fully deserves not only the measured praise of a Grotius, but the enthusiastic exclamations of a Trench. It is " the finest of Christ's parables, filled with true feeling, and painted in the most beautiful colours." It is "the pearl and crown of all the parables of Scripture." Nothing could exceed the chaste perfection of the narrative, the picturesque truth of its portraiture, the psychological delicacy of its analysis. Here is a gem of story-telling, which must be pronounced nothing less than artistically perfect, whether viewed in its general impression, or in the elaboration of its details. We must add to its literary beauty, however, the preciousness of the lesson it conveys before we account for the place it has won for itself in the hearts of men. In this setting of fretted gold, a marvel of the artificer, there lies a priceless jewel; and this jewel is displayed to such advantage by its setting that men cannot choose but see and admire.

Indeed, we may even say that the universal admiration the parable commands has finished by becoming in some quarters a little excessive. The message which the parable brings us is certainly a great one. To lost sinners like you and me, assuredly few messages could appeal with more overwhelming force. Our hearts are wrung within us as we are made to realize that our Father in heaven will receive our wandering souls back with the joy with which this father in the parable received back his errant son. But it is an exaggeration to represent this message as all the Gospel, or even as the core of the Gospel; and to speak of this parable therefore, as it has become widely common to speak of it, as " the Gospel in the Gospel," or even as the summation of the Gospel. It is not that. There are many truths which it has no power to teach us that are essential to the integrity of the Gospel: nay, the very heart of the Gospel is not in it. And, therefore, precious as this parable is to us, and priceless as is its message, there are many other passages of Scripture more precious still, because their message enters more deeply into the substance of the Gospel. Take this passage for example : " For God so loved the world, that He gave His only begotten Son, that whosoever believeth on Him should not perish, but have everlasting life." Or this passage : " God, being rich in mercy, for His great love wherewith He loved us, even when we were dead through our trespasses, quickened us together with Christ (by grace have ye been saved), and raised us up with Him and made us sit with Him in the heavenly places with Christ Jesus." Or even this short passage : " For the Son of Man came to seek and to save that which was lost." All these are more precious passages than the parable of the lost son, not merely because they tell us more fully what is contained in the Gospel, but because they uncover to us, as it does not, what lies at the heart of the Gospel.

It is important that we should recognize this. For the exaggerated estimate which has been put upon this parable has borne bitter fruit in the world. Beginning with an effort to read into it all the Gospel, or at least the essence of the Gospel, it has ended by reading out of the Gospel all that is not in the parable. And thus this parable, the vehicle of a priceless message, has been transformed into the instrument of a great wrong. The worst things are often the corruption of the best : and the attempt to make the parable of the lost son the norm of the Gospel has resulted, I will not say merely in the curtailment of the Gospel,—I will say rather in the evisceration of the Gospel. On this platform there take their stand to-day a growing multitude the entire tendency and effect of all of whose efforts it is to eliminate from Christianity all that gives it value in the world, all that makes it that religion which has saved the world, and to reduce it to the level of a merely natural religion. " The Christianity of the prodigal son is enough for us," they declare : and they declare this with gusto because, to put it briefly, they do not like the Christianity of the Bible or the Christianity of Christ, and are happy not to find them in the parable of the lost son.

Now, let us recognize frankly at the outset, that the reason why these new teachers of an unchristian Christianity do not find Christianity in the parable of the lost son is, briefly, because this parable does not set forth Christianity, but only a small fragment of Christian teaching. The turn they have given to affairs is therefore merely the nemesis that treads on the heels of the mistaken attempts to read a full Christianity into this parable. The parable was not given to teach us Christianity, in its essence or its sum. It was given to teach us one single truth : a truth of the utmost value, not only full of emotional power, but, when placed in its relation to other truths, of the highest doctrinal significance ; but not in itself sufficient to constitute Christianity, or even to embody its essence. How little what this parable teaches us can be conceived as of itself Christianity may easily be made plain by simply enumerating some of the fundamental elements of Christianity which receive no expression in it : and this negative task seems to be made incumbent on us at the outset of any study of the parable by the circumstance of its perversion to the uses of the propaganda of unbelief.

We observe, then, in the first place, that there is no atonement in this parable. And indeed it is precisely because there is no atonement in this parable that it has been seized upon by the modern tendency to which we have alluded, as the norm of the only Christianity it will profess. For nothing is more characteristic of this new type of Christianity than that it knows and will know nothing of an atonement. The old Socinians were quick to perceive this feature of the parable, and to make use of it in their assault upon the doctrine of Christ's satisfaction for sin. See, they cried, the father in the parable asks no satisfaction before he will receive back his son : he rather sees him afar off and runs to meet him and gives him a free and royal welcome. The response is no doubt just that other Scriptures clearly teach the atonement of which no hint is given here ; and that we have no " right to expect that every passage in Scripture, and least of all these parables, which exist under necessary limitations in their power of setting forth the truth, shall contain the whole circle of Christian doctrine." This answer is sufficient against the Socinian who appealed to Scripture as a whole and required to be reminded that we " must consider not what one Scripture says, but what all." But it scarcely avails against our modern enthusiast who either professedly or practically would fain make this parable the embodiment of all the Christianity he will profess. For him, Christianity must do without an atonement, because it is quite obvious that there is no atonement in this parable.

Nor is that more than the beginning of the matter. It must do without a Christ as well. For, we must observe, the parable has as little of Christ in it as it has of an atonement. The Socinians neglected to take note of this. In their zeal to point out that there is no trace in the parable of a satisfaction offered to the Father by which alone He might be enabled to receive back the sinner, they failed to note that neither is there trace in it of any mission of a Son at all—even merely to plead with the wanderer, make known the Father's continued love to him, and win him back to his right relation to the Father. That much of a mission of Christ they themselves confessed. But it is as absent from the parable as is the expiating Christ of the Evangelicals. In truth, there is in the parable no trace whatsoever of a Christ, in any form of mission. From all that appears from the narrative, the errant son was left absolutely alone in his sin, until, wholly of his own motion, he conceived the idea of returning to the Father. If its teaching is to be the one exclusive source of our Christianity we must content ourselves therefore with a Christianity without Christ.

Nor is even this by any means all. For, as has no doubt been noted already, there is as little trace of the saving work of the Holy Spirit in the parable as of that of Christ. The old Pelagians were as quick to see this as were the Socinians later to observe the absence of any hint of a sacrificial atonement. See, they said, the prodigal moves wholly of his own power : there is no efficient grace here, no effectual calling, no regeneration of the Spirit. And there is not. If this parable is to constitute our Christianity, then our Christianity must do without these things.

And doing without these things, it must do without a Holy Spirit altogether. For there is not the slightest hint of a Holy Spirit in any conceivable activity he may be thought to employ in the whole parable. Reduce the mode and effect of His operation to the

most attenuated possible. Allow Him merely to
plead with men from without the penetralium of their
personality, to exercise influences upon them only of
the nature of persuasion, such as men can exercise
upon one another—still there is no hint of such influences here. From all that appears, the prodigal
suo motu turned to the Father and owed to no one so
much as a suggestion, much less assistance, in his
resolve or its execution. If our Christianity is to be
derived from this parable only, we shall have to get
along without any Holy Spirit.

And even this is only the beginning. We shall have
to get along also without any God the Father. What !
you say,—the whole parable concerns the father !
But what a father is this ? It is certainly not the
Father of the Christian revelation and not the Father
of the Christian heart. He permits his son to depart
from him without apparent emotion ; and so far as
appears he endures the absence of his son without a
pang,—making not the slightest endeavour to establish
or maintain communication with him or to recover
him either to good or to himself. If he manifests joy
at the happy return of the son after so many days,
there is not the least evidence that in all the inter-
vening time he had expended upon him so much as a
single message, much less brought to bear upon him
the smallest inducement to return. In other words,

what we know as the " seeking love of God " is absolutely absent from the dealing of the father with the
son as here depicted : that is, the love of God which
most nearly concerns you and me as sinners is con-
spicuous only by its absence. In this respect the
parable stands in its suggestions below the companion
parables of the lost sheep and the lost coin. When
the shepherd lost his sheep, he left the ninety and nine
in the wilderness and went after the lost one until he
found it. When the woman lost her coin, she lit a
candle and swept the house and sought diligently
until she found it. But in the parable of the lost son,
the father is not pictured as doing anything of the sort.
The son leaves him and the son returns to him ; and
meanwhile the father, so far as appears, goes about his
own affairs and leaves the son to go about his. So
clear is it that this parable was not intended to embody the whole Gospel and does not contain even its
essence. For what is the essence of the Gospel if it is
not the seeking love of God ?

The commentators, of course, have not left it so.
Determined to get the Gospel out of the parable, they
diligently go to work first to put it in. Thus one, in
depicting the father's state of mind, grows eloquent
in his description of his yearning love. " He has not
forgotten his son, though he has forgotten him. He
has been thinking of him during the long period of his

absence. Probably he often cast glances along the road to see if perchance the erring one was returning, thinking he saw him in every stranger who made his appearance. He has continued looking, longing, till hope deferred has made the heart sick and weary to despair." Now no doubt the father felt all this. Only the parable does not tell us so. And it would not have omitted to tell us so, if this state of mind on the father's part entered into the essence of its teaching. The fact is that this commentator is rewriting the parable. He is not expounding the parable we have, but composing another parable, a different parable with different lessons. Our Lord, with His exquisitely nice adjustment of every detail of this parable to His purpose, we may be sure, has omitted nothing needed for the most poignant conveyance of the meaning He intended it to convey. That the expositor feels it necessary to insert all this merely proves that he is bent on making the parable teach something foreign to it as it stands. What he has especially in mind to make it teach proves, as we read on, to be the autonomy of the human will. The lost thing, in the case of this parable, is a man : and because he is a man, and no lifeless thing nor an unthinking beast, we are told, he cannot, like the coin and the sheep, be sought. He must be left alone, to return, if return he ever does, wholly of his own motion and accord. Therefore, forsooth, the father's solicitude can only take the form of a waiting ! *Seeking* love can be expended on a coin or a sheep, but not, it seems, on a man. In the case of a man, *waiting* love is all that is in place, or is possible. Is this the Gospel ? Is this the Gospel even of these three parables ? When we were told of the shepherd seeking his sheep, of the woman searching for her coin, was it of sheep and coins that the Master would have His hearers think ? Does God care for oxen, or was it not altogether for our sakes that these parables too were spoken ?

Into such self-contradictions, to say nothing of oppositions to the very *cor cordis* of the Gospel, do we fall when we refuse to be led by the text and begin to twist it like a nose of wax to the teaching of our own lessons. The fact is, the parable teaches us none of these things and we must not bend or break it in a vain effort to make it teach them. Even when another commentator more modestly tells us that the two earlier parables—those of the lost sheep and the lost coin—set forth mainly the seeking love of God ; while the third—that of the lost son—" describes rather the rise and growth, responsive to that love, of repentance in the heart of man " ; he has gone far beyond his warrant. Why say this parable teaches the rise and growth of repentance " responsive to the seeking love of God " ? There is no seeking love of God in the

parable's picture of the relation of the father to the
lost son, as indeed had just been allowed, in the assignment of the teaching as to that to the preceding
parables.   But why say even that it describes " the
rise and growth of repentance " ?   It does of course
describe the path which one repentant sinner's feet
trod as he returned to his father : and so far as the
case of one may be the case of all, we may therefore be
said to have here, so far as the narrative goes, a typical
instance.   But there is no evidence that this description was intended as normative, and certainly no
ground for finding in this the purpose of the parable.
That purpose the text itself places elsewhere ; and
our wisdom certainly lies in refusing to turn the
parable into allegory, reading into it all sorts of lessons
which we fancy we may see lurking in its language
here and there.   We are safest in strictly confining
ourselves to reading out of it the lesson it was designed
to teach.   This lesson was certainly not " the growth
and course of sin " and " the growth and course of
repentance " ;   but simply that " there is joy in
heaven over one sinner that repenteth."   The exquisite
surety of our Lord's touch as He paints the career of
the unhappy man whose fortunes He employs to point
His moral may tempt us to look upon the vivid
picture He draws as the normative instance of sin and
repentance : and surely there is no reason why we

should not recognize that the picture thus brought before us corresponds with remarkable closeness to the great drama of human sin and repentance. But one must be on his guard against being led astray here. After all, the descriptions and analyses in the parable are determined directly by the requirements of the story, not by those of the history of the sinful soul over against its God ; and we must beware of treating the parable as if its details belonged less to the picture than to something else which it seems to us adapted to illustrate. The only safe course is strictly to confine ourselves to the lesson the parable was framed to teach.

This is not to say, however, that this lesson is so single and simple that we can derive no teaching from the parable beyond what is compressible into a single proposition. It undoubtedly has its main lesson ; but it could not well teach that lesson without teaching along with it certain subsidiary ones, closely connected with it as corollaries and supports, or at least implicated in the manner in which it is taught. Only, we must be very wary that we do not either on the one hand confuse these subsidiary things with the main lesson of the parable, or on the other read into it lessons of our own, fancifully derived from its mere forms of expression. We may perhaps illustrate what we mean and at the same time gather the teaching we

may legitimately derive from the parable by asking ourselves now seriously what we do really learn
from it.

And here, beginning at the extreme circumference
of what we may really affirm we learn from this parable,
I think we may say that we may derive from it, in the
first place,—in its context, in the way it is introduced
and in its relation to the fellow-parables coupled with
it—one of those subtle evidences of the deity of our
Lord which are strewn through the Synoptic Gospels.
Although it leads us away from our main course, it
behoves us to pause and take note of this, in view of
the tendency lingering in some quarters to deny to the
Synoptic Gospels a doctrine of the deity of Christ, and
especially to the Jesus of the Synoptics any real
divine consciousness. It would seem impossible for
the unprejudiced reader to glance over these parables
in their setting without feeling that both the evangelist
and the Master as reported by him speak here out of
an underlying consciousness of His divine claims and
estate. For, note the occasion out of which these
parables arose and the immediate end to which they
are directed. The publicans and sinners were flocking
to the gracious preaching of Jesus, and Jesus was so
far from repelling them, that He welcomed them to
Him and mixed in intimate intercourse with them.
This the Pharisees and Scribes made the subject of

unpleasant remark among themselves. And our Lord spoke these parables in defence of Himself against their attack. But now note how He defends Himself. By parables of a good shepherd seeking his lost sheep ; of a distressed woman seeking her lost coin ; of a deserted father receiving back his wayward child. We surely do not need to argue that the good shepherd, the distressed woman, the deserted father stands in each instance for God. Jesus Himself tells us this in His application : " I say unto you " (and we must not miss here the slight but majestic intimation of the dignity of His person) " that there shall be joy in heaven " ; " Likewise, I say unto you there is joy before the angels of God." Yet these parables are spoken to vindicate not God's, but Jesus' reception of sinners. The underlying assumption that Jesus' action and God's action are one and the same thing is unmistakable : and no reader fails tacitly to recognize Jesus Himself under the good shepherd and the distressed woman and the deserted father. In Him and His action men may see how things are looked upon in heaven. The lost, when they come to Him, are received because this is heaven's way ; and since this is heaven's way, how could *He* do otherwise ? This is not a mere appeal, as some have supposed, to the sympathy of heaven : as if He would say to the objector, " I have not your sympathy in this, but

heaven is on my side ! " Nor is it a mere appeal to a
future vindication : as if He would say, " Now you
condemn, but you will see it differently after a while."
It is a defence of His conduct by reference of it to its
true category. These publicans and sinners—why,
they are His lost ones : and does not in every sphere
of life he who loses what he values welcome its recovery with joy ? Throughout the whole discussion
there throbs thus the open implication that He bears
the same relation to these sinners that the shepherd
does to the sheep lost from the flock, the woman does
to a coin lost from her store, the father does to a
wandering child. And what is this but an equally
open implication that He is in some mysterious way
that Divine Being against whom all sin is committed,
away from whose smile all sinners have turned, and
back to whom they come when, repenting of their sin,
they are recovered to good and to God ?

In these parables, then, we see Jesus teaching with
authority. And His divine voice is heard in them also
rebuking sin. For the next thing, perhaps, which it
behoves us to take notice of is the rebuke that sounds
in them of the sin of spiritual pride and jealousy. This
rebuke of course culminates in the portrait of the elder
son and his unsympathetic attitude towards the rejoicing over his brother's return home, which occupies
the latter part of the parable of the lost son. This

episode has given the expositors much trouble ; but this has been occasioned solely by their failure to apprehend aright the purpose of the parable. It is in truth an integral part of the parable, without which the parable would be incomplete.

In the former two parables—those of the lost sheep and the lost coin—Jesus was directly justifying Himself for " receiving sinners and eating with them." His justification is, shortly, that it is precisely the lost who require His attention : He came to seek and to save the *lost*. But these parables run up into a higher declaration : the declaration that there is joy in heaven over one sinner that repents rather than over ninety and nine just persons who need no repentance. This high note then becomes the dominant note of the discourse : and it is to illustrate it and to give it vividness and force in the consciousness of His hearers that the third parable—that of the lost son—is spoken. This third parable has not precisely the same direct apologetic purpose, therefore, which dominates the other two. It becomes more didactic and as such more of a mirror to reflect the entire situation and to carry home to the questioners the whole involved truth. Its incidents are drawn from a higher plane of experience and the action becomes more complex, by which a more varied play of emotion is allowed and a more complicated series of lessons is suggested. It is, therefore, not content, like the former parables, merely to illustrate the bare fact that joy accompanies the finding of the lost, with the implication that as sinners are what is lost to God, it is their recovery which causes Him joy. It undertakes to take up this fact, already established by the preceding parables, and to fix it in the heart as well as in the mind by summoning to its support the deepest emotions of the human soul, relieving at the same time the free play of these emotions from all interference from the side of a scrupulous sense of justice.

It is this latter function which the episode of the elder brother subserves ; and it appears therefore not as an excrescence upon the parable, but as an essential element in it. Its object is to hold up the mirror of fact to the Pharisaic objectors that they may see their conduct and attitude of mind in their true light. Their moving principle was not, as they fancied, a zeal for righteousness which would not have sin condoned, but just a mean-spirited jealousy which was incapable of the natural response of the human spirit in the presence of a great blessing. They are like some crusty elder brother, says our Lord, who, when the long-lost wanderer comes contritely home, is filled with bitter jealousy of the joyful reception he receives rather than with the generous delight that moves all human hearts at the recovery of the lost.

The effect, you see, is to place the Pharisaic objectors themselves in the category of sinners, side by side with the outcasts they had despised ; to probe their hard hearts until they recognized their lost estate also ; and so to bring them as themselves prodigals back in repentance to the Father's house. That they came back the parable does not say. It leaves them in the midst of bitter controversy with the Father because He is good. And here emerges a wonderful thing. That " seeking love " which is not signalized in the parable with reference to the lost—the confessedly lost—son, is brought before us in all its beautiful appeal with reference to these yet unrepentant elder brothers. For, you will observe, the father does not wait for the elder brother to come into the house to him ; he goes out to him. He speaks soothing words to him in response to his outpouring of bitterness and disrespect. When, in outrageous words, this son celebrates his own righteousness and accuses the father of hardness and neglect, refusing indeed in his wrath to recognize his relationship either with him or his : the father responds with mild entreaties, addressing him tenderly as " child," proffering unbroken inter-course with him, endowing him with all his possessions, —in a word, pleading with him as only a loving father can. Did the elder son hearken to these soft reproofs and yield to this endearing appeal ? It was for the

Pharisees to answer that question. Our Lord leaves it there. And the effect of the whole is to show them that, contrary to their assumption, the Father in heaven has no righteous children on earth ; that His grace is needed for all, and most of all for those who dream they have no need of it. By thus skilfully dissecting, under the cover of the sour elder brother, the state of mind of the Pharisaic objectors, our Lord breaks down the artificial distinction by which they had separated themselves from their sinful brethren, and in doing so breaks down also the barriers which held their sympathies back and opens the way to full appreciation by them of the joy He would have them feel in the recovery of the lost. Was there one among them with heart yet open to the appeal of the seeking God, surely he smote his breast as he heard these poignant closing words of the parable and cried, no longer in the voice of a Pharisee, but in the voice of the publican, " God be merciful to me a sinner ! " Surely, like one of their own number only a few years later, the scales fell from his eyes and he confessed himself not only a sinner, but even the chief of sinners.

It would not be quite exact perhaps to say that the parable rebukes spiritual pride and jealousy as well as proclaims the joy in heaven over the recovery of the lost. Its lesson is one ; and its one lesson is only thrown into a clearer light by the revelation of the dreadfulness of its contrast in jealousy of the good fortune of the saved. When all are in equal need of salvation, where is there room for censorious complaint of the goodness of God ? This levelling effect of the parable raises the question whether there is not contained in it some hint of the universalism of the Gospel. Surely through and through its structure sounds the note of, " For there is no difference ! " No difference between the publicans and sinners on the one side, and the Pharisees and the Scribes on the other. The Pharisees themselves being judges, this were equivalent to no difference between Jew and Gentile. Were not the publicans to them as heathen men ? And was not " sinners " just the name by which they designated the Gentiles ? If their scrupulous attention to the law did not raise them above all commerce or comparison with sinners, what profit was there in being a Jew ? We certainly do not purpose to say with some that Jesus was teaching a universal religion without knowing it : and we certainly do not discover here the germ of a universal religion in this—that Jesus meant to teach that nothing lies between the sinner and his recovery to God but an act of the sinner's own will, an act to which every sinner is ever competent, at all times and in all circumstances. And yet it seems not improper to perceive in the levelling effect of the implied inclusion of the Pharisees themselves in the one great class of sinners a hint of that universalism which Jesus gave His Gospel when He proclaimed Himself the Saviour of all who believe on Him.

But, however this may be, we approach nearer to the great lesson of the parable when we note that there is certainly imbedded in its teaching that great and inexpressibly moving truth that there is no depth of degradation, return from which will not be welcomed by God. A sinner may be too vile for any and every thing else ; but he cannot be too vile for salvation. We observe at any rate that our Lord does not hold His hand when He comes to paint the degradation of sinners, through His picture of the degradation into which the lost son had sunk. No depths are left beneath the depths which He here portrays for us. This man had dealt with his inheritance with the utmost recklessness. He had wasted the whole of it until he was left stripped bare of all that he had brought from his father's house. Nor was there anything to take its place. The country in which he had elected to dwell was smitten, throughout its whole extent, with a biting famine. In all its length and breadth there was nothing on which a man might live. The prodigal was reduced to " bend and pray and fawn " at the feet of a certain citizen of that dread land ; and was sent by him out into the barren fields

—to feed swine ! To a Jew, degradation could not be more poignantly depicted. Yes, it could : there was one stage worse and that stage was reached. The lost son not only herded the swine ; he herded with them. " He was fain to fill his belly from the husks that the swine did eat." Not with the same quality of food, observe, but from the swine's own store—for " no man gave unto him." In this terrible description of extreme degradation there may be a side glance at the actual state of the publicans, our Lord's reception of and association with whom was such an offence to the Jewish consciousness. For did not they not merely serve against their own people those swines of Gentiles, but actually feed themselves at their trough ? But however this may be, it is clear that our Lord means to paint degradation in its depths. He does not spare the sinners with whom He consorted. His defence for receiving them does not turn upon any failure to recognize or feel their true quality ; any representation of them as not so bad after all ; as if they had been painted blacker than they were, and were nice enough people to associate with if only we were not so fastidious. He says rather that they are bad past expression and past belief. His defence is that they can be saved ; and that He is here to save them. Lost ? Yes, they are lost ; and there is no reason why we should not take the word at the top—or rather at the bottom—of its meaning : this is the parable of the *lost* son. But Jesus is the Saviour of the lost ; and there is none so lost that he may not be found by Him, and, being found by Him, be also found in Him. Oh, no ! Jesus does not rejoice in sinners : it is not sin He loves nor sinners as sinners. What He rejoices in is the rescue of sinners from their sin. And the deeper the sin the greater the rescue and the greater the joy. " I say unto you, there is joy before the angels of God over one sinner that repenteth." " I say unto you, there shall be joy in heaven over one sinner that repenteth, rather than over ninety and nine just persons, such as have no need of repentance."

It is in this great declaration that the real purport of the parable is expressed. This parable was spoken to teach us, to put it briefly, that God in heaven rejoices over the repentance of every sinner that repents. It is a commentary therefore on those great passages which tell us that God would have no man perish, but all to come to Him and live ; and it is more than a commentary on these passages, inasmuch as it throws the emphasis upon the positive side and tells us of the joy that God feels at the repentance of every sinner who repents. To the carrying of this great message home to our hearts all the art of the parable is directed, and it is our wisdom to read it simply to this end. We need not puzzle ourselves over the significance, then, of this detail or that, as if we were bound or indeed permitted to discover, allegorically, some spiritual meaning in each turn of the story. The most of these find their account in the demands of the story itself and enter into its lesson only as contributory details, adding vividness and truth to the illustration.

Thus, for instance, if we ask why there are only two sons in the parable, while there were ten pieces of silver in the preceding one, and a hundred sheep in the first one ; the answer is that just two sons were needed to serve Jesus' purpose of illustrating the contrast between the Pharisees and Scribes on the one side and the publicans and sinners on the other ; his purpose not being at all to indicate proportion of numbers, but difference in status and conduct. In the former parables the suggestion of comparative insignificance was requisite to bring out the full lesson ; in this, the contrast of character serves His purpose. If again it is asked why it is the younger son who becomes a prodigal, the answer is that the propriety of the story demands it. It would be inconceivable that the older son, who according to custom was the co-possessor and heir of the fundamental estate, should have asked or received an inheritance apart from it. But the thing was not unnatural, and doubtless not unusual, in a younger son, who was to be portioned off in any event in the end, and was only asking that he might not wait on his father's death, but might be permitted to " set up for himself " at once. We cannot therefore with confidence discover the beginnings of the prodigal's downfall in his request that his inheritance might be told off to him, or wonder overmuch why the father so readily granted this request. It is tempting, no doubt, to see in the wish of the son to " set up for himself " a hint of a heart already little at one with the law and custom of the father's house. But such allegorizing is dangerous, especially when not suggested by any hint in the language of the narrative or necessarily contained in the situation depicted. It is customary to speak of the younger son as a young man. It may be so. But the narrative does not say so. He may have been in middle life ; and it may well have seemed to all con- cerned that a desire on his part to begin to build up his own house was altogether right and fitting. The separation of his goods from his father's at all events appears in the parable only as the precedent condition of his spending them, not as the beginning of his downfall.

We need not go further, however, into detail. Enough that the story has a single point. And that point is the joy of the father at the return of the son, a joy which is the expression, not of the natural love of the father for a son, but of the overwhelming emotion of mingled relief and thankfulness and over-mastering rapture which fills the heart of a father on the recovery of a lost son. The point of the narrative is not, then, that this prodigal is a son, though that underlies and gives its verisimilitude to the picture. The point is that this son is a prodigal. It is because he has been lost and is now found that the joy of the father is so great. The elder son is a son too ; and the father loves him also. Let him who doubts it read again the exquisite narrative of the father's tender and patient dealings with him. There is not in all literature a more beautiful picture of parental affection pleading with unfilial passion. This father knew perfectly how to fulfil the injunction later laid down by the apostle Paul : " And ye fathers, provoke not your children to wrath ; but nurture them in the chastening and admonition of the Lord." From this point of view that soothing admonition, " Child, *thou* " (the emphasis on the " thou " must not be neglected) " art always with me ; and all that is mine is thine ; but it was meet to make merry and be glad, because this thy brother was dead and is alive, and was lost and is found "—is simply perfect. So clear is it that the lesson of the parable does not turn on the prodigal's being a son, but on this son being a prodigal.

In other words, its lesson is not that God loves His children, but that God loves sinners. And thus this parable is seen ranging with the preceding ones. The lost sheep, the lost coin, the lost son, have only this one thing in common, that they are lost ; and the three parables unite in commending the one common lesson to us, that as men rejoice in the recovery of what is lost, so God rejoices in the recovery of sinners —since sinners are the things that to Him are lost. We must not, then, use this parable to prove that God is a father, or draw inferences from it as if that were its fundamental teaching. It does not teach that. What it teaches is that God will receive the returning sinner with the same joy that the father in the parable received the returning prodigal ; because as this son was to that father's heart above all other things that he had lost, his lost one, and his return was therefore above all other things that might have been returned to him his recovery ; so sinners are above all else that God has lost in the world His lost ones, and their return to Him above all other restorations that may be made to Him His recovery. The vivid picture of the father not staying to receive the returning son, but, moved with compassion as he spied him yet a great way off, running out to meet him and falling on his neck and kissing him in his ecstasy again and again ; cutting short his words of confession with the command that the best robe be brought to clothe him, and shoes for his blistered feet, and a ring for his finger, and the order that the fatted calf be killed and the feast be spread, and the music and the dance be prepared—because, as he says, " This my son was dead and is alive, was lost and is found "—all this in the picture is meant to quicken our hearts to some apprehension of the joy that fills God's heart at the return of sinners to Him.

O brethren, our minds are dulled with much repetition, and refuse to take the impression our Lord would make on them. But even we—can we fail to be moved with wonder to-day at this great message, that God in heaven rejoices—exults in joy like this human father receiving back his son—when sinners repent and turn to Him ? On less assurance than that of Jesus Christ Himself the thing were perhaps incredible. But on that assurance shall we not take its comfort to our hearts ? We are sinners. And our only hope is in one who loves sinners ; and has come into the world to die for sinners. Marvel, marvel beyond our conception ; but, blessed be God, as true as marvellous. And when we know Him better, perhaps it may more and more cease to be a marvel. At least, one of those who have known Him best and served Him most richly in our generation, has taught us to sing thus of His wondrous death for us :

That He should leave His place on high,
And come for sinful man to die,
You count it strange ?—so do not I,
    Since I have known my Saviour.

Nay, had there been in all this wide
Wide world no other soul beside
But only mine, then He had died
    That He might be its Saviour ;

Then had He left His Father's throne,
The joy untold, the love unknown,
And for that soul had given His own,
    That He might be its Saviour !

Is that too high a flight for us—that passion of appropriation by which the love of Jesus for me—my own personal soul—is appreciated so fully that it seems natural to us that He, moved by that great love that was in Him for me—even me—should leave His throne that He might die for me,—just me,—even were there none else beside ? At least we may assent to the dispassionate recognition that in the depths of our parable is hidden the revelation of that fundamental characteristic of Jesus Christ by virtue of which He did become the Saviour at least of sinners. And seeing this and knowing ourselves to be sinners, we may acknowledge Him afresh to-day as our Saviour, and at least gratefully join in our passionate sinner's prayer :

And oh ! that He fulfilled may see
The travail of His soul in me,
And with His work contented be,
    As I am with my Saviour !

Yea, living, dying, let me bring
My strength, my solace from this spring,
That He who lives to be my King,
    Once died to be my Saviour !

JESUS ONLY

ACTS iv. 12 :—And in none other is there salvation : for neither is there any other name under heaven, that is given among men, wherein we must be saved.

JESUS ONLY

A NOTABLE miracle had been wrought. As Peter and
John were entering the temple at the hour of after-
noon prayer, they had encountered a poor cripple who
was in the habit of having himself laid at the gateway
to beg alms of the passing worshippers. Him they
had healed, attracting his attention and faith by the
great word, " In the name of Jesus Christ the Nazarene,
walk ! " To the confounded crowd that ran together
Peter had improved the opportunity to preach Jesus,
whose mighty name, on faith having been awakened
in it, had wrought this wonderful cure. The Sadducean
leaders of the people had been, as the narrative puts
it, greatly " worked up " by the occurrence ; and,
apprehending Peter and John, they had cast them
into prison overnight and brought them on the morrow
before the Sanhedrin. The question put to the apostles
in their examination before this body was studiedly
insulting in its every phrase, and runs up into an
explosion of angry contempt : " What sort of power
is it, and what sort of a name is it that you have done
this thing by—you ? " There is here an open relega-
tion of the apostles to that herd of " vagabond Jews "
who infested every city, working strange things by

the power of some great name which they pronounced in their incantations.

" Then Peter," says the narrative, " filled with the Holy Spirit, said to them : ' Rulers of the people, and elders, if it can possibly be we ' "—note the emphasis of personal protest in this " we,"—" ' who are to-day called to account, for a good deed ' "—note this emphatic " good deed " ; not the misdeed for which it is customary to call men to account—" ' to an infirm man, by what it is that he has been saved,—be it known to all of you and to the whole people of Israel ' " —here Peter it will be seen is rising to his climax,— " ' that it is by the name of Jesus Christ the Nazarene, whom ye ' "—an emphatic " ye " locating the persons with clear and strong assertion—" ' whom *ye* crucified, whom God raised from the dead,' "—oh, the tremendous poignancy of that contrast !—" ' by this name it is that he stands before you whole. This is the stone that was despised by you the builders, that is become the head of the corner.' "

Assuredly, we will say, pungency of rejoinder, boldness of proclamation, could go no further. And there stood the healed man in their midst, the living witness of the truth of the declaration. But Peter does go further than even this. Not content with so ringing an assertion of the reversal in the court of heaven of their earthly verdict on Jesus the despised Nazarene, and of the living presence among them of Him whom they had foully slain, doing wonders, Peter now suddenly rises to the height of his great argument and sets His Master on the pinnacle of His glory as the sole Prince and Saviour of all the earth. " This," he says, " is the stone that was set at nought by you the builders, that has been made the head of the corner, and in none other," he adds,—" in none other is there salvation ; for neither is there any other name under heaven given among men, by which we must be saved ! "

It is too late now to speak of the fine note of defiance, of holy and chastened challenge, that rings in this trumpet-like speech of Peter's. In these last words it has passed beyond defiance and even beyond challenge, and taken on the note of summons and high proclamation. In them Peter steps forth unabashed before the world, as the herald of the Prince of Life, and asserts His crown prerogatives. Into the face of the sneering Sanhedrin before whom he stands arraigned he, an unlearned and ignorant man, flings this great and sweeping declaration : that Jesus Christ of Nazareth —whom they had crucified—was not only God's Holy Servant, by way of eminence the Holy and Righteous One, against whom they had therefore grievously sinned when they laid their wicked hands upon Him ; but is actually (though they have slain Him) the very

Lord and Source of Life, into whose sole hands are gathered all the issues of Being, whether in this world or in the world to come.

We must not pause to seek to picture the effect with which this daring predication to Jesus of the unique empire over salvation must have struck upon those Jewish ears that day. Him they had slain, but truly He had risen from the dead to trouble them, and was showing forth His might in signs and wonders done in His name. Here was this crippled man, saved from his infirmity ; and who could gainsay that the cure had been wrought by the name of Jesus ? Nay, here are these unlearned and ignorant men themselves, saved from their special infirmities also ; Peter, for example, who had denied his Lord at the mere glance of a serving-woman, now stands before the Sanhedrin itself, careless of their frowns and his own chains, and boldly proclaims his Lord's risen glory and dominion over the whole realm of life. Who could gainsay that this cure too had been wrought by the name of Jesus ? It is easy to imagine what searchings of heart there were in the Sanhedrin that day ; what marvellings ; what anxious inquiries as to what could be done to stop the spread of such a gospel. The two thousand years that have passed have taught us how vain all their efforts were ; and, having rejected the stone that the Lord had made the head of the corner, how completely was fulfilled in them the further prediction of this same Jesus, that " he that falleth on this stone shall be broken to pieces, while on whomsoever it shall fall it will scatter him to dust."

It is of more importance for us to-day, however, to inquire what we to-day—after these two thousand years of enlightenment during which the gospel of Jesus has had free course and been glorified—should learn from this great declaration of Peter, spoken, we are told explicitly, when he was filled with the Holy Spirit. It assures us too, after so long a time, that there is salvation in none other than Jesus, and that there is no other name under heaven given among men whereby we must be saved. What are we to under-stand by this tremendous assertion ?

We shall be counselled, of course, at the outset, to remember that we have before us here an announce-ment that belongs to the beginnings of the Gospel ; that we are listening to words of Peter, not, say, of Paul or John ; and to words of Peter even, which were spoken before he had been enlightened by the great vision that visited him on the house-top of Joppa. We shall even be counselled to remember that a miracle of physical healing lay at the root of this announcement, and that in its primary meaning, at least, it must be held to bear its natural reference to it. It would be a pity assuredly to forget such things

as these. It is only by bearing them fully in mind
that the large and rich comprehensiveness of Peter's
great declaration can be apprehended. It is true that
the whole situation turns on a miracle of healing ;
that Peter is addressing himself in his entire speech to
a demand for an explánation of the power by which
this physical cure had been wrought ; that he had just
spoken of the healing as a " salvation," making use of
the same word that he employs in this great declaration
itself. He certainly means to declare, and he certainly
does declare, that in none other than Jesus is such
physical salvation to be had ; and that there is no
other name under heaven given among men whereby
they must even thus be saved. Exorcists there were
and healers enough, who pronounced other names
over the afflicted children of men. None of them had
power to save. If ever the evils of this life are to be
relieved, the forces of disease and decay, of injury and
death, to be broken, it will be only by Jesus that it
will be done ; only His name, by faith in His name,
can give that perfect soundness for which we long.
It is doubtlessly equally true that Peter had not yet
wholly sloughed off the hard casing of Jewish exclusiveness that enclosed and straitened his heart. We know
not what elements of crude Messianic hopes may not
have still clung to his thought and conditioned his
conception of salvation. The Jesus whom he pro-

claimed was undoubtedly in his view a king, the fruit of David's loins, and seated upon David's throne ; a prophet aforepromised by Moses and all who came after Moses, now come primarily to Israel that he might bless them first of all, and others, only in and through Israel. He means to proclaim, and he does proclaim, that there is no national Saviour but Jesus, that there is no other name under heaven, given among men, whereby men must be saved from the oppressions of society and the organized life of states. Many other national Saviours had offered themselves and were still offering themselves to his hearers. There was, for example, one Theudas, whom they all remembered, who gave himself out to be a somebody ; and there was Judas of Galilee who only the other day had presented himself to their acceptance. What had become of those that followed after them ? No ; if the yoke of the oppressor is ever to be broken, if society is ever to become that promised kingdom of righteousness for which all long, it will only be by Jesus that it will be accomplished ; only His name, by faith in His name, can bring in the long-expected reign of God.

But it is beyond all possibility of doubt equally true that salvation in Peter's apprehension of it stretched far beyond these conceptions and found its real significance in the things of the spirit. " Remission of sins," and the gift of the Holy Ghost as an inward power making for holiness,—these are the ideas which, at least from Pentecost onward, dominated his thoughts ; the " blotting out of sin " that seasons of refreshing from the presence of the Lord might come—here is expressed the very core of all his longing. No doubt, as regards this spiritual salvation too, he had yet much to learn. No doubt the wideness of God's mercy had not yet been fully revealed in his thought, and no doubt he still expected the Gentiles to become participants in this salvation, not as Gentiles, but only as the result of a spiritual conquest of them by Judaism. But assuredly not the less, but much the more rather, was it therefore inconceivable to Peter that Gentiles could be saved apart from that one Saviour in whom alone was there salvation for even the Jews. That channels of salvation could be open to the " sinners of the Gentiles " which are closed to Jews could not enter his imagination. Any remnants of Jewish exclusivism which may be imagined to have still clung to his thought, cannot be supposed, then, to render it doubtful whether or no the Gentiles too are to be understood to be shut up to this one announced means of salvation, but quite the contrary. " Sinners of the Gentiles," in the very nature of the case, rested in his view under a condemnation indefinitely deeper than the chosen people ; and could hope for salvation only by participation in the blessing which came first to them. So that it must remain beyond all question that Peter's declaration was intended to assert and does assert in the most unqualified and the most exceptionless way possible that in none other than Jesus is this spiritual salvation to be had, and that there is no other name under heaven given among men, whereby men in this sphere, above all, must be saved.

It would seem quite clear, therefore, that to catch Peter's meaning in this great declaration, we must take the conception of salvation in the most comprehensive sense possible for it to bear, and that we must give to his restriction of this salvation to Jesus and His mighty name, the strictest and most stringent interpretation. Doing so, we shall not be subjecting Peter's words to undue pressure, forcing them out of their natural and simple meaning. Rather it is only thus that we can protect them from wresting and preserve to them their natural and simple meaning. Nor can we affect surprise that such is the case. In both matters Peter is here only reflecting in his own way and consonantly with his own personal stage of growth and the circumstances which were determining his language, the common Biblical doctrine.

We certainly shall never do justice indeed to the Biblical conception of salvation taken as a whole, save by giving to that term its widest conceivable

connotation. It may be that we are prone to narrow
and limit it on this side and that, and then to feel
some surprise, perhaps some perplexity, when we open
the pages of Scripture and light upon passage after
passage which will not square with our poor starveling
ideas. In the Biblical conception of it,—we shall not
be able to say it too emphatically—salvation broadens
its beneficent reach to cover every evil that afflicts
the afflicted race of man. And that with the best of
reason. For in the centre of its centre, in the heart of
its heart, salvation is deliverance from sin, and accordingly it is deliverance from all the evils that find their
roots in sin : and every evil of every kind that has ever
entered the sphere of human life is consequent on sin
and but the manifestation of sin's presence and power
in humanity. We open a recent book and find written :
" God Himself cannot prevent the consequences of
sin, the sorrow, disgrace and suffering which are the
direct effect of evil doing." We bless the God and
Father of our Lord and Saviour Jesus Christ, the Lord
of heaven and earth, that such is not the teaching of
this blessed Bible. " They shall hunger no more," we
read, " neither thirst any more ; neither shall the sun
strike upon them, nor any heat, . . . and God shall
wipe away every tear from their eyes . . . and death
shall be no more, neither shall there be mourning, nor
crying, neither shall there be any more pain." Sym-

bolical this language no doubt is, but it is such, nevertheless, because it expresses much more, not less, than
it directly says : and so far as faithfulness to Biblical
teaching goes it could be read with the literalness of a
legal document. The favourite expression for salvation
in the Biblical record is that great word Life ; which is
set over against the equally great word Death, as the
best comprehensive term to gather up all the evils
from which we shall be saved. Whatever Death is,
and all that Death is, and all that leads up to, accompanies and follows Death, in any one of its possible
applications, physical and temporal, spiritual and
eternal—that is what we shall be saved from in this
salvation. And whatever Life is, and all that Life is,
and all that leads up to, accompanies and expresses,
and grows out of and crowns Life—in every possible
application of that great conception—that is what we
shall be saved to in this salvation : or rather that, in
Biblical language, *is* salvation. " In the day that
thou eatest thereof, thou shalt surely die "—in these
terms was couched the great prohibition of " the fruit
of that forbidden tree whose mortal taste," as Milton,
not a whit too comprehensively, puts it, " brought
death into the world and *all* our woe." Everything
that vexes and troubles human life in every sphere of
its manifestation is but the issue of this first dis-
obedience. Conceive man as a physical organism held

together by the subtle forces which govern material
life ; all that brings him pain, disease and death,
emerges as the unavoidable result of sin and therefore
the necessary object of salvation. Conceive him as a
social being bound in fellowship with his companions
by those mutual ties which hold together the fabric of
society ; all that brings him discontent, strife, injustice, oppression, want or neglect, equally truly is
the fruitage of sin and equally truly is therefore the
object of salvation. Or conceive him at the height of
his nature, as a spiritual being standing in relation to
that spiritual world above him which stretches upwards to the throne of God itself ; all that breaks the
free play of this high communion and rouses in him
the sense of incompatibility with his higher environment ; all that rises within him as a bar to that favour
of God which is life, whether in the form of guilt or
corruption,—this above all is the bitter fruit of sin and
therefore above all the immediate object of salvation.
We must conceive salvation as reaching out with its
healing hand to the utmost confines of the effects of
sin, or else fail to recognize with the poet the Restorer
as a " greater man " than him through whom we
suffered this grievous loss. The Scriptures certainly
will not permit us to entertain fancies so derogatory to
the glory of the Redeemer. They do not content
themselves indeed even with an equation of the spheres

in which the forces of destruction and restoration work as if it were enough to say that the gift of life shall supplant the curse of death—following it into all the ramifications of its baneful effects that it may work their reversal. Nay, no sooner have they drawn the parallel than they at once correct it with a fervid, " but *not* as the trespass, so also is the free gift. For if by the trespass of the one the many died, *much more* did the grace of God and the gift by the grace of the one man Jesus Christ *abound* unto the many." There is a superabundance of grace, and an extension of it immeasurably beyond the ravages wrought even by sin.

Would we do justice to the Scriptural representations, then, we must conceive nobly of salvation. We must enlarge its borders if we would give to it all the land which the Lord has promised it. It belongs to the glory of Christ that His salvation enters into every region of human need and proclaims in all alike complete deliverance. Even the lower creation, by virtue of the relation in which it stands to man, partakes in his redemption. If the very ground was cursed for man's sake that the place of his abode might sympathetically partake in his punishment, no less shall it share in his restoration. Man's sighs are not the only expression of the evil that curses human life in its sinful development. The whole creation groans and travails together with him. But it shares also in the hope of the coming deliverance. For there shall be a new heaven, we are told, and a new earth. Under these new heavens, in this new earth, shall gather redeemed humanity, in the perfection of its idea, and in perfect harmony with its perfected environment. In the perfection of physical vigour : for what is sown in corruption shall have been raised in incorruption, what is sown in dishonour shall have been raised in glory, what is sown in weakness shall have been raised in power, what is sown in selfishness shall have been raised in spirituality. In the perfection of social organization and intercourse : for there shall be none to hurt or destroy in all God's holy mountain, and all the people of the Lord shall have learned righteousness. In the perfection of spiritual communion with God : for then it is that the Lord shall make Himself known to His people and shall dwell with them, and they shall need no Temple to which men should require to repair in order to meet the Lord, for the Lord God the Almighty and the Lamb are the Temple thereof, and the grace of the Lord shall flow down the streets in a river of the water of Life washing into every nook and corner. Such is the picture the Scriptures draw for us of the salvation of our God. And let us not fail to note that it is a picture of a saved world. As no sphere of human life is left untouched by it ; as on its touch, every sphere of human life is transformed ; so the completeness and the profundity of its renovation of man is matched by the wideness of its extension over man. It is the renewed heavens and the renewed earth that we are bidden to contemplate ; and dwelling in them in endless bliss renewed humanity. Renewed *humanity ;* not a meagre company withdrawn from the sin-festering race, but the race itself, cleansed and purified and gathered home to the Father's arms ; not without loss suffered by the way, it is true, for there are some who shall not enter into this holy city ; but with all losses made good, all breaks in the ranks filled up, and all lacks and wants supplied by Him who has redeemed it to Himself and led it to its new estate of perfection in itself and eternal communion with Him. Such is the salvation that has been wrought out for us by Christ.

Now the point to which the words of Peter, which are particularly engaging our thought to-day, energetically direct our attention is that neither this salvation as a whole, nor any least part of or element in it, can possibly be attained save in Jesus Christ. " And in none other," he declares with tremendous emphasis, " in none other is there *this* salvation," this well-known salvation which fills all our hopes and longings :—" in none other is there this salvation : for neither is there any other name, under heaven,

given among men, wherein we must be saved." Peter's
interest, we will observe, is absorbed, not in the greatness of the salvation, but in the greatness of Jesus
Christ the Nazarene, who is the Lord and sole disposer
of this great salvation. He assumes that the idea of
this salvation and its indescribable greatness, and an
insistent craving for it, are all present, persistent, con-
trolling in the minds and hearts of his auditors. What
he is concerned with is to carry home to their minds
and hearts the autocracy of Jesus Christ the Nazarene
over it. Hence the negative form given to his declaration. He does not say, you observe, " You ask by
what power or by what name this cure has been
wrought. I reply by the power and name of Jesus
Christ of Nazareth, in whose mighty hands rests
power to heal all the ills of men." No, he gives quite
a different tone to his declaration when he turns forward its negative edge and declares with enormous
energy of expression : " You ask by what sort of
power or by what sort of name we have done this
thing. I reply it is by the name of Jesus Christ the
Nazarene, and there is not in any other this salvation ;
for neither is there another name, under heaven, given
among men by which we must be saved." Observe the
accumulation of emphatic phrases to enhance the stress
laid on the exclusiveness of Jesus' power to save.
First of all, there is the redoubled assertion : " in none

other is there salvation," and then again that none
might miss it, " there is no other name under heaven,
given among men, whereby we must be saved." Then
there is the heaping up of clauses, in almost superfluous reiteration of the absoluteness of the exclusion
of all but Jesus from the power of saving : there is
" none other," there is " no other name," " under
heaven," " given among men "—as if it should be said,
" Seek you wherever men can be found, search to the
utmost limits of the encanopying sky,—nowhere
among men, nowhere under the stretch of heaven's
roof, will you find a whisper of another name in which
salvation can be found." And then, at last, there is the
curious turn given to the phrase : " in which we *must*
be saved." We weaken it vastly in our careless
current reproductions of it, saying, " neither is there
any other name under heaven given among men
wherein we *may* be saved,—wherein we *can* be saved."
Peter does not so phrase it. He says, " wherein we
must be saved." The accent of necessity is in it. It
is not merely that we may be saved by Jesus, or that
we can be saved by Jesus ; but, if we be saved at all,
it *must* be in Him that we are saved. There is no
possibility otherwise or elsewhere. And with the
emergence of this vigorous *must* at the end of the
sentence the last hammer falls, the last rivet is clinched,
and the last band of steel is fixed around this tre-

mendous assertion of the exclusiveness of salvation in Jesus Christ alone.

The note of Peter's declaration here, you will observe, is, " Jesus only ! " " Jesus only ! " There is a note of severity in the mode in which he declares it, for the occasion of its declaration was such as to call for assertion,—assertion in the face of hard unbelief, of persistent denial of the crown-rights of the King. But through all the severity there sounds also a note of exuberance. This is the account to be given indeed of the almost unexampled piling up of phrases to which we have adverted, adding little to one another as they do except an ever-growing emphasis for the main declaration ; expressive in a word only of the overflowing emotion that was flooding the speaker's heart. The name of Jesus was inexpressibly precious to Peter, and it was thus inexpressibly precious to him because it was the saving name, nay, we will not express it adequately until we say it outright—because it was the *only* saving name in all the universe. It was much to him, no doubt, that he had come to perceive that there had been given to that broken and suffering man whom he had seen but yesterday hanging on the cruel cross, the Name that is above every name, that in the name of Jesus every knee should bow, of things in heaven and things on earth and things under the earth, and that every tongue should confess that Jesus

Christ is Lord, to the glory of God the Father. This supreme exaltation of his Master alone must have filled his soul with swelling delight. But there was something beyond this supreme exaltation itself that was suffusing his whole being with unutterable joy. It was the exuberant sense of the uniqueness of Jesus' office of Saviour that pressed for utterance and found it haltingly in an accumulation of phrases that must appear extravagant to all who do not with him rise to the height of the great vision. Jesus exalted to the throne of the universe,—that is a great vision ; but Jesus the sole Lord of salvation, holding in His hands the keys of life, and dividing to each as He will,—Jesus the only Name under heaven given among men whereby man must be saved—to sin-stricken and despairing men, surely this is a much greater vision. It was this greater vision that had caught Peter's uplifted eyes.

Not, of course, as if it were to his eyes alone that it was given to see it. There is nothing that Peter tells us here that is not told us over and over again by every writer of this New Testament. It belongs indeed to the very heart of the Gospel that these writers preached, which centred not precisely in the proclamation of salvation, but in the preaching of Jesus as Saviour. To them indeed Jesus *is* the Gospel ; and where Jesus is not, there there is no gospel at all. It is of the very essence of the Gospel, therefore, that salvation can be

obtained through Jesus alone. And so it was preached
from the beginning. " I am the way, the truth, and
the life," said Jesus Himself as plainly as majestically :
" no man cometh unto the Father, but by Me." And
equally plainly again, in that equally majestic assertion reported to us by Matthew and Luke on which
He founds one of the most touching of His invitations :
" All things have been delivered unto Me by My
Father ; and no one knoweth the Son, save the Father ;
neither doth any know the Father, save the Son, and
he to whom the Son willeth to reveal Him." That as
there is one God, so there is only " one mediator
between God and men, the man Christ Jesus," after
whose once offering of Himself " there remaineth no
more sacrifice for sins," became accordingly the centre
of the Gospel proclamation by His accredited messengers. And therefore they did not hesitate to
proclaim boldly that only they who believe in Jesus
Christ shall be saved : and that those who are without
Christ have no hope and are without God in the
world. The life that God has given us, explains John
in his searching way, is deposited for us " in the Son,"
and therefore, " he that hath the Son hath the life ;
he that hath not the Son of God hath not the life."

It was, in fact, this arrogant exclusiveness of the
Gospel in which its offence in large part consisted.
Even the Jew might have been persuaded to accept

Jesus as a Rabbi, teaching a way to God ; and the Gentiles in that syncretistic age would have welcomed with acclamation such a teacher among the multitude of their other masters. But neither Jesus nor His followers would accept such an assignment. He and they alike claimed for Him the sole empire over salvation and would brook no fellow by his side. When we contemplate the wide liberality of the Roman world, and consider the ease with which the most varied cults found room for themselves side by side in that spacious toleration, we are sometimes tempted to wonder why, among all this crowd of religions, Christianity alone was singled out for violent and indeed relentless persecution. The solution is of course that Christianity was not, and would not consent to be considered, one of these multiform religions. It was and it proclaimed itself to be the one only valid religion ; and, thus pitting itself against them all, it drew the hatred and the assault of all against itself. A recent writer, seeking to draw for us a picture of the exclusive attitude of Christianity in those old days of the beginning of the Gospel, commences with a string of quotations from the great representative writers of the time,—Irenæus and Tatian and Commodian and Tertullian and Cyprian himself, that man of moderate, one might say even politic, spirit, from whom more smooth speech might

have been expected : but wearying of his task he
breaks off suddenly with the remark that to present
the whole case it would be necessary to cite the whole
body of Christian authors, and well-nigh the whole
list of Acts of Martyrs with them—since there is, he
says, no one of them who does not assert the exclusiveness of Christianity. It brought them ridicule ; it
brings us ridicule yet. It brought them persecution of
unexampled ferocity, as it brings us the scorn of man
yet. But in that sign they conquered. Heathenism,
throwing itself upon them with fury, did not break
them : it broke itself upon them. And they have
handed on the banner to us still bearing the unsullied
legend of " Jesus only,"—Jesus the sole author of
salvation.

Now, it is not a popular thing to-day any more than
it was two thousand years ago to assert the exclusiveness of Christianity. Men no longer cast us to the
lions when we proclaim Jesus the only Saviour the
world can know ; His name the only name under
heaven given among men wherein they must be saved.
But the world of to-day endures with no more real
patience than that older world two thousand years
ago the arrogance of such lofty claims. This is above
all others that have preceded it the day of eager and
appreciative study of other faiths ; and equally with
the others that have preceded it, the day of indifference,

if not hostility, to the high claims of Jesus. You will be pressed on every side to give some recognition to the large element of truth and good that is found in the historical religions of the earth ; to the high conceptions of God that are enshrined in some of them, the noble ethical teaching that is the essence of others, the poignant pity for suffering humanity that throbs through others. You will be pressed on every side to accord an appreciative hearing to the voice of the religious spirit speaking in the hearts of men, who, nevertheless, have not learned to express their religious emotions in the formulas with which you have been made familiar. What, you will be asked, will you refuse your welcome to the aspirations of the soul that is naturally Christian ; will you not give hearty recognition to the service that is rendered to the " essential Christ " by thousands who have never heard His earthly name, or who, having heard it, have failed rightly to estimate His unique character ? Will you forget that the man Christ Jesus was the Word of God before He became flesh, and remains through all the ages that Light that lights every man that comes into the world ? Will you dare to deny to His sovereign grace the right to quicken whom He will, under whatever sky and calling on God by whatever human name ; or refuse to recognize the movings of His inspiration in the hearts of men—because, forsooth, they speak not your words and swear not in your symbols ? It will be hard for you to resist the specious pleas with which you will be plied and to preserve in your heart—I will not say now on your lips—the echoes of Peter's great declaration that in none other than Jesus is there salvation, that there is none other name under heaven, given among men, whereby we must be saved.

I beg you, when the temptation to admit other saviours to a place by His side, to acknowledge other names as equally potent with this unique name of Jesus, is strong upon you to remember three things. Remember the great commission : remember the peril of your own souls : remember the honour of Jesus Christ your Saviour.

Remember the great commission ! " All authority is given unto me in heaven and earth," declared our Saviour when He was about to ascend to His throne. " Go ye, therefore," He commanded His disciples, " and make disciples of all the nations." Was this great commission the great mistake of history ? It has required all the heroism the Church could command to make even the tentative efforts she has been able to make to fulfil it ; and every step of the way has been watered by floods of her best blood. Have we now come at last to see it in a clearer light and to understand the error of judgment, or rather the profoundly

deflected point of view, on which it was all founded ?
From our higher standpoint, shall we say that all the
nations are already in the right path, and need no
instruction from us to find the way : that the essential
truth is already in their grasp and they may be trusted
to its guidance : that having thus the leading of the
Logos they cannot fail of the life ? Such clearly was
not our Saviour's view, whom we recognize as the
Logos, to the guidance of whom we would trust the
world, and who proclaimed Himself the Truth indeed, or
He would never have sent His Church upon this—in
that case—useless if not noxious mission. And if such
be our view, we will never go upon this great mission
in which consists, nevertheless, the very reason for the
existence of the Church on earth. Only if we catch
the apostles' view-point, and can say to our souls
with the clearness of conviction which they felt, that
there is salvation in Jesus alone, will we be inspired
with the zeal that filled them, to evangelize the world.
The nerve of the missionary spirit after all is em-
balmed for ever in Paul's great sorites. Only they
that call upon the name of the Lord shall be saved.
" How then shall they call on him in whom they have
not believed ? and how shall they believe in him whom
they have not heard ? and how shall they hear without
a preacher ? and how shall they preach except they
be sent ? " The salvation of the world hangs, thus, in

our human mode of speaking, on the clearness and the strength of our conviction that there is salvation in none other than Jesus, that there is none other name under heaven, given among men, wherein they must be saved. O the cruelty of that indifferentism, mis-called broadness of mind, that would withhold from a perishing world the only healing draught, on the pretence, forsooth, that it is not needed. O remember that the whole world lies in iniquity—ill to death with the dreadful disease of sin,—and that you have in your hands the one curative potion, the only water of life which can purge away sin and restore to spiritual health and beauty. Remember the great commission !

And remember the peril of your own souls ! Jesus Christ has come into the world to save sinners. And He calls you to Him, you who are weary and heavy laden with the burden of your sins. He points you to His wounded hands and feet and to His riven side. He points you to His outpoured blood. He points you to His finished sacrifice and to the Father's great, It is enough ! In Him he proclaims to you there has been opened up at last access to the Father, and to the Father's forgiveness, and to the Father's love He is able to save unto the uttermost all that come unto God through Him. He pleads with you to come. He presses upon you the greatness of the opportunity, the greatness of the peril. He urges you with the great promise : He that believeth shall be saved. He importunes you with the sharp warning : He that believeth not shall be lost. Will you neglect so great salvation, which has at the first been spoken by the Lord, and has been confirmed unto us by those that heard Him, God also bearing witness by the wonders of His grace without us and within ? And all because, forsooth, we cannot believe there is no other way ? Other masters enough will demand your attention ; other teachers essay your guidance. The wisdom of the world will laugh at your narrowness and point you to other ways of approach to God. I charge you, by the welfare of your own souls—and what should a man give in exchange for his soul ?—to bear steadily in mind that the world by its wisdom has never yet attained to the knowledge of God. Where is the wise ? Where is the scribe ? Where is the disputer of this world ? Has not God made foolish the wisdom of this world ? Let those who are set on perishing despise the word of the cross as foolishness. You who are set on salvation —bear it well in mind that it is the power of God unto salvation, apart from which there is no salvation. On the peril of your souls, I charge you to remember that Jesus Christ is the only way, the only truth, the only life ; that no man comes or can come to the Father except by Him, that all the life that is in the world is in Him, and he only that hath Him hath the life, while he that hath not Him hath not the life. Listen to the solemn words of the apostle of love : " Whosoever denieth the Son, the same hath not the Father : he that confesseth the Son," he, and he only, "hath the Father also." Let us note it clearly and note it whole : there is no access to God for sinners save in the blood of Jesus Christ.

Ah, I know what is rising upon your lips to say ! You are of these who have believed in Jesus ; your hearts are full of joy because you find yourselves in Him, and, being in Him, in the enjoyment of His salvation. I charge you, then, brethren, companions of the blessed life, remember the crown rights of your Lord and Saviour ! Let His honour be precious in your sight ! I have charged you in the words of Paul to let no man rob you of your crown : I charge you now in yet more insistent tones, to let no man rob your Saviour of His crown. In Him and in Him alone is redemption. In His hands He holds, as sovereign Lord of salvation, all the issues of life. Being at the right hand of God exalted, and having received of the Father the promised Holy Spirit, it is He and He alone that sheds down on earth all the currents of influence that make for salvation. Say in your heart and shout abroad with your lips, that all men may know it assuredly, that God has made this Jesus both Lord

and Christ, and beside Him there is no other. See to
it that you ever honour Him in your hearts and cease-
lessly proclaim Him with your voice as the one only
Saviour the world can ever have ; since in none other
is there any salvation ; and there is no other name
under heaven given among men, wherein we must be
saved. Only so will you render to Him the glory that
is His due. For when there was no one in the heavens
or on the earth or under the earth who was able to
open the book of salvation or to break the seals thereof,
this man was counted worthy ; worthy to endure the
pangs of death for the offences of men, worthy to rise
from the dead for their justification, worthy to be
exalted to the throne of God and to receive the power,
and riches, and wisdom, and might, and honour, and
glory, and blessing. He by whose hand has been
wrought salvation, He is and remains the only Lord
of Salvation, and beside Him is no fellow. Let this
good confession, I beg you, echo throughout all the
corridors of your life and fill with its voice all the
recesses of your souls. Above even the great commission, above even the peril of your own souls,
remember—remember as those should remember who
owe their all to Him, remember the honour due to
Jesus Christ, the Saviour, the sole Saviour, of this lost
world.

THE LAMB OF GOD

JOHN i. 29:—Behold the Lamb of God, which taketh away the sin of the world.

THE LAMB OF GOD

JOHN the Apostle was the pupil of John the Baptist.
Alone of the evangelists, he had not merely heard the
preaching of this last and greatest of the prophets,
but had formed one of the inner circle of his disciples,
closely attached to his person and intimately acquainted with his entire thought. And he had brought
to this teaching the same receptive and brooding heart,
attuned to the higher truth, which he afterwards
brought to the teaching of Christ. The result was
very much the same. There are scattered here and
there through the sayings of Jesus recorded by the
other evangelists, deep sayings enough to assure us
that, even as they would set it forth, there was this
element in the teaching of the Master ; but John's
record of our Lord's discourses is compacted of these
deep sayings. So there are hints enough in the record
of the Baptist's preaching given by the other evangelists, to make it clear that there was such a side to it
as John records ; but it is John alone who throws this
aspect of it into the foreground. In both alike, the
Baptist is purely the forerunner of the Lord, whose
whole work consisted in making ready for the Lord's
coming. But the attention of the other evangelists is

directed to the pathway prepared for the feet of the
Lord ; John's is focused upon the figure advancing
over the road. They tell us, therefore, of the trumpet-
call to repentance which the Baptist sent ringing
through the land, of his searching inquisition into the
hearts of men, of his unsparing rebuke of evil whether
in high places or in low, of his flaming proclamation of
judgment ; John tells us rather of the testimony of
the Baptist to Christ. From them we learn accordingly
what the Baptist thought of man ; from John, what
he thought of Jesus.

And when we learn from John what the Baptist
thought of Jesus, we are startled by the clearness and
fulness of his prophetic vision. We have already
reminded ourselves that John was a pupil of the
Baptist. Let us now give its full validity to this fact.
At least this much he obviously would himself have us
say,—that all he ever came to know of Jesus he saw,
when he looked back upon the teaching of his first
master, to have been already contained in germ in his
prophetic instruction. It is therefore that he lays
such stress on the testimony of the Baptist to Jesus.
Even from the reports of the Baptist's teaching given
in the other evangelists, we may perceive that he saw
in Jesus a person, and expected of Him a work, which
marked Him out as the divine Saviour of the world.
What is thus implicit in their report, however, is made

explicit in John's. We need not suppose that John fully understood from the beginning all he heard from the Baptist's lips. But, like Mary, he belonged to that class of profound religious natures who are accustomed to hide the deep declarations of the prophets in their hearts, that they may ripen under the influences which the experiences of later life bring. And thus, after John had lain on Jesus' bosom as he had sat at the Baptist's feet, and had drunk from that fuller and richer fountain, he was in a position to tell us that there was included in the Baptist's declaration a true knowledge of Jesus, a knowledge of who and what He was and what He came into the world to do, a knowledge of Him, in the fulness of the meaning of that great designation, as the " Son of God," and, in the fulness of the meaning of that great declaration, as " the Lamb of God, that takes away the sin of the world."

It is easy to say that such fulness of apprehension is incredible in the Baptist. That, standing as he did, in the grey dawn of the new dispensation, it is incongruous to bathe him in the full light of noonday, a noonday which did not shine upon Christ's own disciples until long afterwards—which, indeed, never shone upon them until their Master's work had been accomplished and was bearing its own witness to itself, until He had not only died for our·sins, but risen again for our justification and had sent His Spirit to teach

their laggard understandings things which earlier they
had been unable to bear. Nay, are we not attributing
to the Baptist, it is asked, a knowledge to which even
Jesus Himself attained only slowly, as He learned by
the things which He suffered ; for did not He Himself
begin His ministry animated by the hope of establishing
the Kingdom He came to erect through the mere force
of His winning proclamation, and only gradually learn,
as the cross threw more and more deeply its baleful
shadow over His pathway, that it was only through
suffering that He could attain His glory ? How shall
we believe that to the Baptist there lay open from the
beginning all that the Lord Himself and all His
disciples learned only at the end ; and even, that the
Baptist taught it all, on his prophetic authority, both
to Jesus and to Jesus' disciples, who were his pupils,—
although certainly with so little effect that they forthwith forgot it and required painfully to recover it in
the hard school of experience ? If indeed we must
not even say that the Baptist forgot it himself ; for
how else can we suppose that he could send to Jesus
that perplexed inquiry, " Art Thou He that should
come, or do we look for another ? "

Plausible, however, as such doubts and hesitations
may be made to appear, the answer to them is easy
and decisive. They are utterly without historical
foundation. They are purely the fruit of an attempt to

reconstruct the historical sequences of the evangelical narrative in the interests of an *a priori* theory,—of an *a priori* theory, moreover, the principle of which is rejection of the supernatural factor in the history, though this supernatural factor is no less the nerve of the whole historical development than the very heart of the Christian religion. If we are to credit the evangelical narrative (and what other source of information have we ?) it is not true that our Lord began His ministry with the expectation of accomplishing His mission through the instrumentality of successful preaching alone. Every one of the evangelists represents Him as undertaking His work with a clear perception of precisely what lay before Him ; as coming into the world, in a word, not that He might live and build up a Kingdom, but that He might die and through His death purchase a people to Himself ; as entering from the beginning, that is to say, upon the conscious fulfilment of the programme which the Baptist marked out for Him when He called Him the Lamb of God that takes away the sin of the world. It is true the disciples are represented as, in their preoccupation with another Messianic ideal, slow of heart to believe that it should be thus and not otherwise with their Master, that it should be through the sufferings and death of the cross that He should accomplish His work and enter into His glory. But

the significance for this of the Baptist's preannounce-
ment falls into the background in view of the repeated
declarations of the Lord Himself, running up at last
into careful and precise instruction, which only their
dullness of spirit was able to resist ; and, indeed, in
view of the broad preadumbrations of the Old Testament itself, which the evangelists would have us understand laid down beforehand the entire plan of our
Lord's life.   When the risen Christ turned to His
despondent disciples with the sorrowful rebuke, " O
foolish men and slow of heart to believe all that the
prophets have spoken, ought not the Christ to suffer
these things and to enter into His glory ? " He but
put into direct words once again before He was taken
up the teaching of His whole life, which has become the
teaching of all His biographers as well.

From the point of sight of our Lord Himself and of
these narratives which embalm His memory for us,
there was really nothing new in the Baptist's proclamation and nothing exceptional in it, beyond its designation of the man Jesus as the expected Messiah.   It
was but the summary presentation of the essential
teaching of the Old Testament, and particularly of
that great prophet of whom as truly as of Elijah the
Baptist was a revival, and, in whose prophecies his
testimony, as recorded by John, is steeped.   Little
marvel that those who could forget Isaiah, could forget

also the Baptist's crisp summary of Isaiah's teaching. Little marvel that, in the hour of his own trial, even he himself should sink into a certain measure of despondency and need to reassure himself that He on whose head he had seen the Spirit descend and rest, was really He that should come, and he need not look for another. In the progress alike of the individual and of the Kingdom of God upwards towards those heights of knowledge and privilege which at the start, perchance, stand out clearly in view touched with the glow of sunrise, it often happens that they are temporarily lost from sight as the lower valleys and shaded paths are traversed, by which they are approached. The very process of attaining the fuller possession of them involves the hiding of them for a time from view. There is nothing psychologically unnatural, therefore, either in the clear perception of the Baptist, from the vantage-ground of the opening of the new dispensation, of the true character of the Messiah and the real nature of His work ; or in the evangelist's recalling the fulness of this prophetic teaching after the event had justified it and he had himself through his inspiration attained a firm grasp of its elements. What John, in effect, invites us to do, is to come back with him to the dawn of the Christian proclamation, and to observe with him how this lonely peak was " fired by the red glow of the rushing morn." " Listen," says he to us, "listen, to these marvellous words which fell from the great prophet's lips in the rich flow of his inspiration. When I heard them, then, they kindled a flame in my heart which has not yet died down ; in their impulse I turned and followed Jesus. When I recall them now I see in them nothing less than a direct witness from God to what Jesus was and did. Hearken to them as a voice from heaven, declaring what in truth is the central fact of the Gospel."

So we seem to hear the evangelist speaking to us out of the records of his Gospel this morning, and we would not be disobedient to the heavenly message. Let us, then, ask what it is that the Baptist, thus reported to us, bids us behold in Him whom he declares to be the Lamb of God that takes away the sin of the world.

We remark, then, in the first place, that he bids us see in Jesus the suffering servant of God.

In the preparation for the coming of redemption which forms the main burden of the Old Testament revelation the promised redeemer is presented in a great variety of aspects, corresponding to the multifarious functions which he was to perform as the Saviour of His people. Among these, none fell in so completely with the popular temper, or appealed with such force to the popular imagination, as that

which foretold Him as the Son of David, the great
warrior-king who should subdue the world to the God
of Israel and for ever rule over the whole race of man.
Fired with hopes kindled by this great prediction, the
prevailing conception of the Messiah very naturally
came to be that of a monarch, whose dominion was
inevitably transmuted into a more or less carnal
kingdom of power over the enemies of Israel. Meanwhile the other lines of prophetic description were
neglected ; and among them most of all that culminating in the fifty-third chapter of Isaiah, in which
the Messiah is depicted as the righteous servant of
Jehovah, preserving his integrity amid the contradictions of sinners, and by his patient endurance of
the sufferings inflicted upon Him not merely earning
the favour of God, but purchasing blessings for the
people. What it concerns us to observe now is that
the Baptist, in designating Jesus the Lamb of God
that takes away the sin of the world, recalls his hearers
from the one Messianic ideal to the other. His prophetic announcement is the authoritative designation
of Jesus as the long-expected Messiah, the Hope of
Israel ; but along with that, the authoritative definition of the Messianic ideal to be fulfilled in Jesus, as
very especially that set forth in the figure of the
servant of Jehovah. It is the prophetic proclamation
of the great doctrine of the suffering Messiah, in terms

and tones which imperatively claimed a hearing and admitted no misunderstanding.

In this, indeed, consists the offence of the Baptist's announcement. It was its offence at the time. Had the Baptist come proclaiming the advent of a warrior-king, who should, with the rod of His anger, break in pieces the oppressors of Israel, Herod might still have slain him, but the Pharisees would have believed in Him, and no Jew would ever have questioned whether his mission were from heaven. It remains his offence to the present day. This doctrine of a suffering Messiah, we are asked,—what unheard-of doctrine is this ? No Jew ever dreamed of it, we are told, until he had been taught it by the Christians ; and the Christians invented it only to reconcile the catastrophe which had befallen their Christ with their hope that it would have been He who should redeem Israel. It concerns us little when the Jews, in their engrossment with the expectation of a Messianic King of the earth rather than of heaven, first began to lend tardy ear to the Isaian proclamation of a suffering Messiah ; it is a historical question of some obscurity whose solution has little bearing on our practical life. But it is obvious that the contention that the doctrine of a suffering Messiah was first introduced by the Christians to save the situation when their Messiah succumbed to the machinations of His foes and

poured out His blood at Calvary, involves the complete
rewriting of the New Testament in the interests of an
a priori theory. Here stands written in the forefront
of the Gospel narrative, a crisp proclamation of the
doctrine of the suffering Messiah from the mouth of
John the Baptist ; and over and over again from the
very outset of the narrative of His life it is represented as underlying the announcements of Jesus
Himself, as it is later made the prime topic of His
instruction to His disciples and the staple of the
preaching of all His followers. In very truth, if we
conceive the great religious movement inaugurated by
John the Baptist, and carried through by Jesus and
His followers, from the point of view of the development of the Messianic conception, its significance is
precisely that of a sustained effort to revolutionize the
dominant Messianic ideal,—to substitute for the
conception of Messiah the king of Israel, that of
Messiah the suffering servant of Jehovah. This is
written large over the whole face of the New Testament. Every one of the evangelists as he seeks to
present a vital picture of how Jesus comported Himself on earth, makes his appeal to the fifty-third
chapter of Isaiah, as laying down the programme on
which His life was ordered (Matthew viii. 17, Mark
xv. 28, Luke xxii. 37, John xii. 35 ; also Matthew xi.
5, xii. 18, xxi. 5, Luke iv. 18, etc.). In the didactic

portions of the New Testament this conception is simply carried forward and developed into its doctrinal implications (Rom. x. 16, 1 Peter ii. 22, Acts viii. 28, Rev. v. 6, xiii. 8). The doctrine of the suffering Messiah may thus be truly said to be the nerve of the whole New Testament presentation. There is nothing peculiar, therefore, in the Baptist's proclamation except its initial position at the head of a development which has revolutionized, not the Messianic ideal merely, but the world itself. Historically speaking its entire significance is that it announces in a clear, sharp, startlingly worded proclamation at the very outset of the new dispensation, its whole programme. Precisely what characterizes the New Testament most profoundly as the documentation of a movement issuing from the bosom of Judaism is its ideal of the Messiah as the suffering servant of Jehovah. Precisely what differentiates Christianity most sharply from the Judaism from which it issued is its proclamation of this Messianic ideal. Precisely the distinction of the Baptist is his initial announcement of this altered hope.

" Behold," cries the Baptist, pointing to Jesus,— " behold the Lamb of God, which taketh away the sin of the world." In that meek and lowly figure passing yonder, in bearing so simple and unassuming amid His fellow-men, see the Hope of Israel, the Chosen of

God. Lay aside your national passions, your fierce chafing under the foreign yoke ; man suffers from something worse than political bondage or alien oppression ; there is a higher deliverance than that from the dominion of the stranger. It is not a king you need so much as a redeemer ; and the God of our fathers knows it. Behold, there is the Lamb of God which takes away the sin of the world. To his first hearers, that is substantially what the proclamation of the Baptist meant. To us, to-day, it means, that if we would know Jesus, we must dismiss from our minds all preconceived notions of what it behoved the Lord of all the earth to be, and how it behoved Him to bear Himself in the world, and, under the Baptist's direction, go to the fifty-third chapter of Isaiah and read in that prophetic picture what Jehovah's righteous servant was and how He lived in the earth. And certainly it is no attractive portrait, as men count attractiveness, that the prophet draws of Him. " His visage," he writes, " was so marred, more than any man, and his form more than the sons of man." " He hath no form nor comeliness ; and when we see Him, there is no beauty that we should desire Him." " He was despised and rejected of men," we are told, " a man of sorrows and acquainted with grief ; and as one from whom men hide their face He was despised and we esteemed Him not." "He was stricken, smitten of men, and afflicted "

—wounded, bruised, chastised, oppressed, led like a lamb to the slaughter, put to grief. Epithet is piled upon epithet almost beyond measure, to convey to us a sense of the depth of His humiliation. This, says the prophet to us,—this is our Redeemer. If we would see Jesus as He was, looking beneath the appearance to the actual reality and faultless truth, the Baptist tells us to look at Him in this portrait,—subjected, to put it shortly and sharply, to the most fathomless humiliation that ever befell or will ever again befall a sentient, feeling, palpitating being in all God's universe. There never has been, there never will be, another to stoop as He stooped. You know how Paul put it, seeking to suggest the depth of the humiliation by the interval between that which He was by nature and that which He became by His condescension. God on His throne—a broken slave on the cross ; these are the end terms. As God, He was the Lord of all the earth ; when He became man, He became servant to the whole world ; and not content with that, being found in fashion as a man, He humbled Himself still further even unto death itself, and that the death of the cross. Enough : words cannot paint this humiliation. We read the prophetic portrayal in the fifty-third chapter of Isaiah ; we read the historical portraiture in the pages of the Gospels, culminating in the agony of Gethsemane and the anguish of the

Passion ; we read the dogmatic representation in the arguments of the Epistles. They fill our minds with wonder ; they wring our hearts with compassion ; but we remain conscious through all that even the bloody sweat of Gethsemane and the forsaken cry on the cross are an insufficient index of the soul-anguish which was endured by this greatest of earth's sufferers, this most humiliated of all those who from the primal curse have trodden with bloody feet the thorny surface of this sin-smitten world of ours. Surely the Baptist was right when he bade us see in this Jesus, the type of all righteous sufferers, the suffering servant of Jehovah.

But a great deal more is to be said of this sufferer than merely that He stands before us as the type of all sufferers. His sufferings were not endured for their own sake ; nor did the Baptist suppose that they were. We need to remark, in the second place, there-fore, that the Baptist bids us see in Jesus the sub-stitutive sacrifice for sin.

" Behold the Lamb of God," cries the Baptist, " which taketh away the sin of the world." Not, Behold the Prophet like unto Moses, whom ye shall hear ; nor yet, Behold the Israelite without guile, in whom meet perfect purity, wisdom and truth ; nor even, Behold the Lion of the tribe of Judah, who shall scatter your foes and deliver you from all your enemies.

He might have said any one or all of these things.
They are all true of Jesus. Christ is our teacher, and
our example, and our king. But there is something
more fundamental than any of these things ; something which underlies them all and from which they
acquire their value. And it is this that the Baptist
saw in Christ and sends us to Christ to find. " Behold,"
says he, " the Lamb of God, which taketh away the
sin of the world." That image could mean but one
thing to an humble, sin-conscious Old Testament
saint. He would think first of the righteous sufferer
of the fifty-third chapter of Isaiah : and that righteous
sufferer is not merely described there, we will remember,
as a lamb that is led to the slaughter, and as a sheep
that before her shearers is dumb, the very embodiment
of meekness and patience in enduring the violence of
the despoiler ; but, in well-remembered words which
throw a glory over these sufferings to which even
meek patience and uncomplaining endurance can lend
nothing, we read : " Surely he hath borne our griefs
and carried our sorrows ; he was wounded for our
transgressions, he was bruised for our iniquities ; the
chastisement of our peace was upon him, and with
his stripes we were healed." " All we like sheep have
gone astray ; we have turned, every one, to his own
way ; and the Lord hath laid on him the iniquity of
us all." " For the transgression of my people was he

stricken . . . yet it pleased the Lord to bruise him. He hath put him to grief : when thou shalt make his soul an offering for sin, he shall see his seed, he shall prolong his days, and the pleasure of the Lord shall prosper in his hand. . . . By his knowledge shall my righteous servant justify many, and he shall bear their iniquities. . . . He bare the sin of many and made intercession for the transgressors.'' And along with the fifty-third chapter of Isaiah, the Old Testament saint, when directed to the Lamb of God which takes away sin, would inevitably think also of the paschal lamb, the fundamental national symbol of deliverance ; along with it, beyond question, also of the lamb of the daily sacrifice and of the underlying significance of the whole sacrificial system, with its typical finger pointing forward to something better,— to God's own Lamb, who should really take away sin, a lamb of God's providing, able and willing to bear on his own head the sin of the world.

It is through the eyes of such an Old Testament saint that we of these later days may hope to catch for ourselves the Baptist's meaning. Men have no doubt wearied themselves with efforts to derive from his declaration some less explicit reference to sacrifice. Jesus might well be compared to a lamb, it has been said, merely because of His mild and inoffensive disposition, the gentleness of His bearing, the patience of

His demeanour under the injuries of His foes ; and
He might well be said to take sin away from the world
with reference merely to His zeal for purity of conduct
and heart, the loftiness of His ethical character, the
winning example of the holiness of His life. It may
certainly be doubted whether those who take this line
of remark, have fully understood Jesus—whether they
remember the sternness of His demeanour in the
presence of sin, the excoriation of His rebuke, that
scourge of cords with which He drove the traders from
the Temple, that bearing which, when He set his face
to go up to Jerusalem, caused even His followers to
draw back from Him afraid, leaving Him to rush on
alone in the van. We must beware, because Jesus is
described as bearing with patience the sufferings He
came to endure, of picturing Him therefore to ourselves
as without the power of indignation or without the
will to use it. And it may equally be doubted whether
those who suppose that the sin of the world may be
taken away by any power of persuasion or example,
rightly understand man, or his love of sinning, or the
power of sin in him. But let all this pass. The
artificiality of such attempts to explain away the plain
significance of the Baptist's declaration is too glaring
to require formal refutation. Jesus is not merely compared with a lamb in it ; He is identified with a
specific and particular lamb,—the well-known " Lamb

of God." And whether this be taken as Isaiah's lamb of the fifty-third chapter of Isaiah, or the passover lamb, or the lamb of the common sacrifices, it is in each and every case a sacrificial lamb which is indicated. Nor is Jesus said here in some broad and general way to take away sin. He is said to be the sin-bearer as the Lamb of God : and there is but one way in which from the beginning of the world, or in any nation, a lamb has ever been known to bear sin, and that is, as a piacular sacrifice, expiating guilt in the sight of a propitiated God. The Lamb of God which takes away sin, is and can be nothing other than the lamb of God's providing upon whose head sin is laid, and by whose blood expiation is wrought.

When, then, the Baptist pointed out Jesus as the Lamb of God who takes away the sin of the world, he pointed Him out as the divinely provided sacrifice for sin : he pointed Him out as the substitute for sinners, by whose stripes they are healed. Thus he preached beforehand the Gospel of the blood of Jesus—that blood of Jesus by which alone can our sins be washed away. Following his direction, we shall see in Jesus not merely and not primarily our prophet and not merely and not primarily our king—our prophet and our king though we adoringly recognize Him as being, by whom alone we are effectively instructed in the truth, or protected from the most intimate enemies of our peace and safely directed in our way. Nay, we shall recognize in Him not merely our priest who represents us before God and makes satisfaction for our sins ; but before all and above all, as our sacrifice, —the victim itself upon whose head our sin is laid, and by whose outpoured blood our guilt is cleansed. It is, in a word, the Gospel of the cross—of the cross of Christ—which the Baptist commends to us here ; that Gospel, not only of Christ *simpliciter*, but of Christ as crucified, which has ever remained to the Jews a stumbling-block and to Gentiles foolishness, but which has also ever remained, and will ever remain, to the called themselves, Christ the power of God and the wisdom of God. The blood of Jesus,—O, the blood of Jesus !—when we have reached it, we have attained not merely the heart, but the heart of the heart of the Gospel. It is as a lamb as it had been slain, that He draws to Himself most mightily the hearts, as He attracts to Himself most fully the praises of His saints.

But not even in this high testimony is the witness of the Baptist exhausted. We reach its height only when we remark, in the third place, that he calls upon us to see in Jesus the Saviour of the world.

" Behold," he cries, " the Lamb of God, which taketh away the sin of the world,"—not " our sin " merely, though we praise God that may be gloriously true ; nor " the sin of His people " merely, though that too, when properly understood, expresses the entire fact ; but, with clear vision of the ultimate issue, " the sin of the world." The propitiatory sacrifice which the Baptist sees in Jesus, is a sacrifice of world-wide efficacy : the salvation which he perceives to issue from it stretches onward in its working until it embraces the whole world. The sin of the world, as a whole, he gathers, as it were, into one mass ; and, laying it upon the head of Jesus, cries, " Behold the Lamb of God, which taketh away the sin of the world." It is in this universalism, we say, that we reach the height of the Baptist's declaration.

And it is in this universalism that it has become common to discover the element in the Baptist's proclamation which is specifically new. The suffering Messiah, it is often said, is no doubt an Old Testament doctrine ; Messiah the sin-bearer, yes, even that may be found in the fifty-third chapter of Isaiah : but Messiah the bearer of the sin of the world,—was it not reserved to the opening of the new dispensation, characterized by spiritual breadth, and to John the Baptist, harbinger of Christ, to give explicit expression to this great truth ? It will be well, however, to walk warily even here. The narrowness of the ordinary Jewish outlook cannot, perhaps, be easily overstated, —the pride of the Jews as the special favourites of heaven, and their ingrained determination to confine

the grace of God to the limits of their own nation. But
they certainly were never encouraged in this restricted
view of the reach of God's mercy by the revelation of
His purposes which Jehovah had made to them. From
the moment when He promised to the mother of all
living a seed by whose bruised heel the serpent's head
—the source of all evil in the world—should be crushed,
the extension of His grace was never confined within
narrower limits than the race itself. The normative
promise to the father of the faithful,—typical of all
the other promises of redemption that fill the Old
Testament,—was that in his great Seed (for He saith
not seeds, as of many, but Seed, as of one) should all
the nations of the earth be blessed. Least of all in this
wonderful chapter of Isaiah to which the Baptist's
words carry us most immediately is the sacrifice of
the righteous sufferer circumscribed in its efficacy by
the cleansing of the sins of Israel. " When He shall
have made His soul an offering for sin," we read, " He
shall justify many " ; and, bearing the sins of many,
" so shall He sprinkle many nations." No doubt the
Baptist's declaration, in the springing growth of
prophetic annunciation, goes beyond even this, and
asserts not a relative but an absolute universalism.
Not many nations, but the whole world, is what he
bids us see redeemed in Christ : the Jesus he proclaims as the God-provided sacrifice bears upon His

broad and mighty shoulders nothing less than the world's sin.

It is the note, then, of pure universalism, we perceive, that is sounded in the Baptist's great proclamation. He does not think, of course, of denying that salvation is of the Jews. This Lamb of God was a Jew of the Jews, and came as the Hope of Israel : and only as the Hope of Israel does He become also the Hope of the world. No more does He think of doubting that only as it should work its way out from Israel, perhaps by slow and even tentative stages, could this redemption of Israel extend into and throughout the world. We cannot credit him, to be sure, with detailed foresight of the actual process by which the salvation in Jesus has been conveyed to the world : through the scattering of the disciples from Jerusalem, the preaching of Paul and his companions, the slow missionary advance of the Church and slower leavening of the ingathered mass, through all these two thousand lagging years—and no one knows how many more thousands of years the secular process must continue before the great goal is attained and the great promise fulfilled that the whole shall be leavened. But the Baptist certainly expected the redemption he saw in its potency in Jesus to take effect only through the process of discipling ; and accordingly he directs his own disciples to Jesus that they might attach them-

selves to Him whose very nature it was to "increase,"
and he himself remains through life an interested
observer of the work and career of Him whose pathway
it was his own highest ambition to smooth. Least of
all does the Baptist ever think of obscuring that dark,
that terrible fact, that as the redemption in Jesus thus
makes its way surely to its ultimate goal of the salvation of the world, there are multitudes of sinners
left to this side and that, out of the direct line of its
advance ; there are many who fail to hear the call ;
there are many who hearing refuse to hearken to it ;
there are whole masses of men that are extruded in
the progress of the perfecting whole to its consummate
end. Though the progress be continuous, therefore,
and the goal sure, yet so long as it is progress to a goal
as yet unreached, there must ever remain among the
saved, unsaved—dross amid the gold, chaff to be
winnowed out from the wheat. This Saviour, accordingly, whom the Baptist proclaims as the Lamb of
God who takes away the sin of the world, he presents
also as the husbandman who prunes and weeds His
garden, and cuts down the unfruitful trees to cast
them into the flames ; as the Lord of the harvest who
has His fan in His hand and thoroughly purges His
threshing-floor, burning up the chaff with unquench-
able fire. The Baptist neither denies nor glozes such
things as these. But neither does he focus his eye

upon them as if they were the end which Jesus had in view in coming into the world. Rather, looking through and beyond them, he fixes his gaze upon the ultimate goal which, after the process attended by these effects is over, shall at length be attained, and in this great declaration points to Jesus as bearing in His own body on the tree nothing less than the sin of the world.

You will observe, that what I am endeavouring to do, is to make as plain as I can that the Baptist's gaze, when he declares that Jesus takes away the sin of the world, is directed to the end of a process—a process of long continuance and of varied appearance through the several stadia of its course. He sees in Jesus the Saviour of the world and perceives in Him a saved world. Through the turmoil and the labour which accompany the accomplishment of this great task ; through the long years of progress towards the goal, the centuries and millenniums of but partial success and oft-times even of apparent failure, which we know as the history of the Church and which even we (let us praise God for it) can recognize as the history of the expansion of Christianity ; he looks out upon the end, that end to which all has been steadily advancing, when the knowledge of the glory of the Lord shall cover the earth even as the waters cover the sea,— with the same breadth and expansion, leaving no nook or cranny unfilled, and with the same depth of fulness, overwhelming all. It is the spectacle of a saved world thus which fills his vision. And with this spectacle full in his eye, he may well afford to neglect all that intervenes, and to proclaim Jesus simply as the Lamb of God that takes away the world's sin. He is unquestionably the husbandman who prunes His garden well, and casts the improfitable plants and branches to the flames : but on that very account He is not a Husbandman who gives over His garden—the garden of the Lord—to thorns and weeds and unfruitful trees, but rather one who cleanses it and makes it in effect— this very garden in its entirety—what it has in principle been from the beginning, is now, and ever shall be, the Garden of the Lord in which shall grow at last, luxuriantly filling it in its whole extent, only plants of worth and trees of delight. He is beyond doubt the winnower of men, whose fan is in His hand, to beat out the chaff and cast it in the fire : but on this very account He does not give over His threshing-floor to the worthless and cumbering chaff, but thoroughly purges it that, after the chaff is burned, it may remain the garner of the Lord heaped with the precious grain. Accordingly the Baptist does not teach us that in Jesus the sin of the world is so taken away in the mass, that there has not been and shall not yet be in the process by which the world has been and is being saved

by Him, unfruitful trees cut down and chaff cast into
the fire ; but rather that in the end, when the process
is over, no unfruitful trees will be found growing in
God's garden, the world, no chaff be found cumbering
God's threshing-floor, the world. The vision he brings
before us, let us repeat it, is the vision of the ultimate
salvation of the world, its complete conquest to Christ
when at last Jesus' last enemy shall have been conquered and the whole world shall bow before Him as
its Lord and its Redeemer. On the basis of this great
consummation seen hanging on the margin of the
future by his prophetic eye, he declares of Jesus that
He bears in His body on the tree the whole world's
sin, and in very truth is to be acclaimed as the Saviour
of the World.

Such, then, is the Jesus to whom the Baptist would
direct our eyes, when he bids us behold in Him the
Lamb of God that takes away the sin of the world.
Let us not fail to derive at least two great lessons from
his exhortation.

The first of them is this : we must never despair of
the world. This is certainly a much-needed lesson.
For are we not very prone to despair of the world ?
And is there not very good apparent reason why we
should despair of it ? For who can deny that the world
is very evil ? Only, we must not add in the words of
the old hymnist, that therefore " the times are waxing

late." This world is not to rot down into destruction, but to become, however slowly and by whatever tentative processes, the very garden of the Lord. That the world is very evil is no proof, then, that the times are waxing late ; but, if any inference can be drawn from it, the contrary rather. The world has always been very evil, ever since there entered it, through that forbidden fruit, the sin of man and all our human woes. Throughout all the ages, its sin has gone up reeking before God to heaven. Viewed in itself we could not but despair of it. But the great fact—the great fact, greater even than the fact of the world's sin—is that Christ has redeemed this sinful world. In Him we behold the Lamb of God which takes away the sin of the world. Not, who strives to take it away and fails ; not, who takes it away in some measure, but is unable to take it away entirely ; not, who suspends its taking away upon a gigantic *IF*—as though His taking it away were dependent on some aid given Him by the world itself—that world which loves its sin and will never give it up of itself and which will, of course, always act when left to itself in accordance with its nature as the sinful world. No, but who actually, completely, finally, takes away its sin. This,—I beg you to bind the great truth on your heart,—this, despite all appearances that smite the astounded eye and the slowness of its realization

of its great destiny—is a redeemed world, in which we
live. It has been purchased unto God by the most
precious blood of His Son. Its salvation, in God's
own good time and way, can no more fail than the
purpose of God can fail, than the blood of Jesus Christ
can be of none effect. God's ways, to be sure, are not
as our ways : there is none of us fitted to be His coun-
sellor ; we cannot review His plans nor bid Him stay
and justify to us His methods of working. It must
ever remain a mystery to us why He works in this
world by process ; why He created the world by
process, why He has peopled it by process, why He
has redeemed it by process, why He is saving it by
process—by process so slow and to our human eye so
uncertain, cast so much to the mercy of the currents
that flow up and down through the earth, that we are
tempted at times to doubt whether it is directed to a
goal at all. We know only that it is by process that
God chooses to work in the world,—except this further :
that, though He works by process, He ever gloriously
attains His ends. This wicked world in which we live
is, then, God's world, Christ's world ; it belongs to
Christ by right of purchase and nothing can snatch it
out of His hands. The day will surely come when the
kingdoms of the world shall become the kingdom of our
God and His Christ ; and we—you and I—are co-
workers with God in bringing about the great con-

summation. O lift up your eyes from the dust and noise of the strife and its apparently fitful fortunes, and, shall I not even say ? doubtful issue ; and under the direction of the Baptist, fix them upon the end : lift them from the world's sin and its just doom for its sin, to the world's Saviour and its abounding life in Him. See the redeemed world in its redeeming Lord, clothed in righteousness ; and let your hearts beat high with the vision and gather courage for your daily tasks as messengers of God to a world lost indeed in its sin, but found again in its Saviour.

The second lesson is : we must not despair of ourselves. Living in this sinful world, as constituent members of it, we are partakers of its sin ; or, as it may be more fair to put it, its sinfulness is but the expression of our sin. How can we, sinners, cherish hope of life ? In ourselves, surely, we can find no ground for such a hope : and that we know right well. Our hearts condemn us and God is greater than our hearts. If we look at ourselves, how can we not despair ? Let us look, therefore, not at ourselves but at Jesus ; for Jesus, the Baptist tells us, is the Lamb of God which takes away sin. And, note it well, troubled heart, the Baptist did not make this declaration to those who had no sin, or even to those who, having it, knew not that they had it. What appeal, in fact, could such a declaration make to such men as that ? He made it to those whom he had called with flaming speech to repentance ; and who, with burning hearts, had come to his baptism of remission of sin. The message is, then, to you too whose hearts are sore with the sense of sin. To you and me also he cries to-day : " Behold the Lamb of God, which taketh away sin." Is it not a joyful message to sin-stricken souls ? Let others think of Jesus as they may. Let them hail him as a king : let them sit at His feet as a prophet : let them eagerly seek to follow in His steps. For you and me, sinners, He is most glorious and most precious, as a Saviour. Let others make elaborate inquisition into the possible reasons which led Him to come into this sinful world of ours. He Himself tells us that there were but two reasons which could have brought Him into the world—to judge the world, or to save the world. And, blessed be His name, He has further told us that it was actually to save the world that He came. This is the only reason that can satisfy our hearts, or even our reason, —that Jesus Christ came into the world to save sinners. It is only as the Lamb of God that has been slain, to purchase unto God by His blood of every tribe and tongue and people and nation, and to make them unto God a kingdom and priests who shall reign on the earth,—that the heavenly hosts in the apocalyptic vision hymn Him ; and it is only as we catch a glimpse of this His true glory that we can worthily add our voices to His praise. It is only when we see in Him a slaughtered lamb, lying on a smoking altar, from which ascends the sweet savour of an acceptable sacrifice to God for sin, that we can rise to anything like a true sense of the glory of Jesus Christ, or in any degree give a sufficing account to our souls of His presence in the world.

> " *The Lord has come into His world !* "
>   Nay, nay, that cannot be ;
> The world is full of noisomeness
>   And all iniquity :
> He is the Lord of all the earth—
> How could He stoop to human birth ?
>
> " *The Lord has come into His world !* "
>   A slaughtered Lamb I see,
> A smoking altar on which burns
>   A sacrifice for me !
> O blessed Lord ! O blessed day !
> He comes to take my sin away !

GOD'S IMMEASURABLE LOVE

JOHN iii. 16 :—For God so loved the world, that He gave His only begotten Son, that whosoever believeth on Him should not perish, but have eternal life.

GOD'S IMMEASURABLE LOVE

To whom we owe this great declaration of the love of God, it is somewhat difficult to determine ; whether to our Lord Himself, or to that disciple who had lain upon His bosom and had imbibed so much of His spirit that he thenceforth spoke with his Master's voice and in his Master's words. Happily it is a matter of no substantial importance. For what difference does it make to you and me whether the Lord speaks to us through His own lips, or through those of His servant, the Apostle, to whom He had promised, and to whom He had given, His Holy Spirit to teach him all the truth ? What concerns us is not the instrumentality through which the message comes, but the message itself. And what a great message it is,—the message of the greatness of the love of God ! Let us see to it that, as the words sound in our ears, it is this great revelation that fills our hearts, fills them so full as to flood all their being and wash into all their recesses. The greatness of the love of God, the immeasurable greatness of the love of God !

This exhortation is not altogether superfluous. Strange as it may sound, it is true, that many— perhaps the majority—of those who feed their souls

on this great declaration, seem to have trained themselves to think, when it falls upon their ears, in the
first instance at least, not so much of how great, how
immeasurably great, God's love is, as rather of how
great the world is. It is the world that God loves,
they say,—the world : and forthwith they fall to
thinking how great the world is, and how, nevertheless,
God loves it all. Think, they cry, of the multitudes
of men that swarm over the face of the earth ; and
have swarmed over it through all the countless generations from the beginning ; and will swarm over it in
ever-increasing numbers through perhaps even more
countless generations yet to come, until the end : and
God loves them all, each and every one of them, from
the least to the greatest ; so loves them that He has
given His only begotten Son to die for them, for each
and every one of them—and for each and every one
of them with the same intent,—the intent, namely,
that he may be saved. O how great the love of God
must be to embrace in its compass these uncounted
multitudes of men ; and so to embrace them that
every individual that enters as a constituent unit into
the mass of mankind receives his full share of it, or
rather is inundated by its undivided and undiminished
flood !

Certainly this is a great conception. But it is just
as certainly not a great enough conception to meet

the requirements of our text. For, look you, will you measure the immeasurable greatness of God's love by the measure of man ? All these multitudes of men that have lived, do live, or shall live, from the beginning to the end of the world's entire span,—what is their finite sum to the infinitude of God ? Lo, the world, and all that is in the world,—and all that has ever been in the world or can ever be in the world,— lies as nothing in the sight of the Infinite One, floats as an evanescent particle in His eternal vision. How can we exalt our conception of the greatness of the divine love by thinking of it as great enough to embrace all this ? Can we praise the blacksmith's brawn by declaring it capable of supporting a mustard-seed on an outstretched palm ? This standard is too small : we cannot compute such masses in terms of it. Conceive the world as vastly as you may, it remains ever incommeasurable with the immeasurable love of God.

And what warrant does the text offer for conceiving so greatly of the world, or indeed for thinking of it at all under the category of extension, as if it were its size that was oppressing the imagination of the speaker, and its parts—down to the last analysis— that were engaging his wondering attention ? Evidently the text envisages the world, of which it speaks in the concrete, as a whole. This world is made up of parts, no doubt, and the differing destinies that await the individuals which compose it are adverted to. But the emphasis does not fall upon its component elements, as if their number, for example, could form the ground of the divine love, or explain the wonder of its greatness. Distribution of it into its elements and engagement with the individuals which compose it, is merely the result of the false start made when the mind falls away from contemplating the immensity of the love of God with which the text is freighted, to absorb itself rather in wonder over the greatness of the world which is loved.

And having begun with this false step it is not surprising if the wandering mind finds itself shortly lost in admiration not even of the greatness of the world, but rather of the greatness of the individual soul. These souls of men, each and every one of which God loves so deeply that He has given His Son to die for it,—what great, what noble, what glorious things they must be ! O what value each of us should place upon this precious soul of ours that God so highly esteemed as to give His Son to die for it ! A great and inspiring thought, again, beyond all doubt : but, again, obviously not great enough to be the thought of the text. Clearly, what the text invites us to think of is the greatness of the love of God, not the greatness of the human soul.

And how can we fancy that we can measure the

love of God by what He has done for each and every
human soul ? Persist in reading the text thus dis-
tributively, making " the world " mean each and
every man that lives on the earth, and what, after all,
does it declare that the love of God has done for them ?
Just open a way of salvation before men, give them an
opportunity to save themselves. For, what, in that
contingency, does the text assert ? Just this : that
" God so loved the world "—that is, each and every man
that has lived, does live, or shall live in this world,—
" that He gave His only begotten Son, that *whosoever
believeth on Him* should not perish, but have eternal
life." " Whosoever believeth on Him,"—those only.
Is this, then, the measure of the immeasurable love of
God—that He barely opens a pathway to salvation
before sinful men, and stops right there ; does nothing
further for them—leaving it to their own unassisted
initiation whether they will walk in it or not ? Surely
this cannot be the teaching of the text ; and that, for
many reasons,—primary among which is this : that
we all know that the love of God has done much more
than this for multitudes of the children of men, namely,
has not merely opened a way of salvation before them,
but has actually saved them. Nor is our text silent
on this point. It is not in this mere opening of a way
of salvation before each and every man that the love
of God for the world is declared by it to issue, but in

the actual saving of the world. We read the next verse
and we discover it asserting that God sent His Son into
the world for this specific end, that the world should
be " saved by Him." God did not then only so love
the world as to give it a bare chance of salvation : He
so loved the world that He saved the world. And
surely this is something far better : and provides a
much higher standard by which to estimate the greatness of God's love.

We discover, then, that the distribution of the term
" world " in our text into " each and every man " in
the world not only begins with the obvious misstep of
directing our attention at once rather to the greatness
of the world than to the greatness of God's love and
only infers the latter from the former ; but ends by
positively belittling the love of God, as if it could
content itself with half-measures,—nay, in numerous
instances, with what is practically no measure at all.
For if it is satisfied with merely opening a way of
salvation and leaving men to walk in this way or not
as they list, the hard facts of life force us to add that
it is satisfied with merely opening a way of salvation
for multitudes to whom it should never be made known
that a way of salvation lay open before them, although
their sole hope lies in their walking in it. And why
dwell on special cases ? Shall we not recognize frankly
that so meagre a provision would be operative in no

case ? For even when it is made known to men that a
way of salvation is opened before them—can they,
being sinners, walk in it ? Let our passage itself tell
us. Does it not explicitly declare that every one that
doeth ill hateth the light and cometh not to the light ?
And who of us does not know that he, at least,—if not
every man,—doeth ill ? Does the love of God expend
itself then in inoperative manifestations ? Surely not
so can be measured the love of God, of which the
Scriptures tell us that its height and depth, and length
and breadth pass knowledge : of which Paul declares
that nothing can separate us from it, not death, nor
life, nor angels, nor principalities, nor things present,
nor things to come, nor powers, nor height, nor depth,
nor any other creature : of which he openly asserts,
that if it avails to reconcile us with God, through the
death of His Son, much more shall it avail to bring us
into the fruition of salvation by His life.

Obviously, then, the distribution of the notion
" world " in our text into " each and every man " in
the world, does less than justice to the infinitude of
the love of God which it is plainly the object of the
text to exalt in our thought. Reacting from the
ineptitudes of this interpretation, and determined at
all costs to take the conception of the love of God at
the height of its idea, men of deeper insight have
therefore suggested that it is not the world at large

that is in question in the text, but God's people, the
chosen of God in the world. Surely, it is God's seeking, nay, God's finding love that is celebrated here,
they argue ; the love which goes out to its object with
a vigour which no obstacle can withstand, and, despite
every difficulty, brings it safely into the shelter of its
arms. The " world " that God so loved that He gave
His Son for it,—surely that is not the " world " that
He loved so little as to leave it to take or leave the Son
so given, as its own wayward heart might dictate ;
but the " world " that He loved enough, after giving
His Son for it, prevalently to move upon with His
quickening Spirit and graciously to lead into the
offered salvation. The " world " of believers, in a
word, as they are called in the following clause ; or, as
they are called elsewhere in Scripture, the " world "
of God's elect. It was these whom God loved before the
foundations of the world with a love beyond all expression great and strong, constant and prevailing, a
love which was not and could not be defeated, just
because it was *love*, the very characteristic of which,
Paul tells us, is that it suffereth long, is not provoked,
taketh no account of evil, beareth all things, endureth
all things, yea, never faileth : and therefore was not
and could not be satisfied until it had brought its
objects home.

It is very clear that this interpretation has the

inestimable advantage over the one formerly suggested, that it penetrates into the heart of the matter and refuses to evacuate the text of its manifest purport. The text is given to enhance in our hearts the conception of the love of God to sinners : to make us to know somewhat of the height and depth and length and breadth of it, though truly is passes knowledge.   It will not do, then, as we read it to throw limitations around this love, as if it could not accomplish that whereto it is set.   Beyond all question the love which is celebrated is the saving love of God ;   and the " world " which is declared to be the object of this love is a " world " that is—not merely given an opportunity of salvation—but actually saved.   As none but believers—or if you choose to look at them *sub specie æternitatis*, none but the elect—attain salvation, so it seems but an identical proposition to say that it is just the world of believers, or the world of the elect, that is embraced in the love of God here celebrated. When the text declares, therefore, that God so loved the world that He gave His only begotten Son for it, is not what is meant, and what must be meant, just the elect scattered throughout the world ?   It may seem strange to us, indeed, to speak of the elect as " the world."   But is not that largely because, in the changed times in which we live, we do not sufficiently poignantly appreciate or deal seriously enough with

the universalism of Christianity, in contrast with the
nationalism of the old dispensation ? In this universalistic and anti-Jewish Gospel of John, especially, what
more natural than to find the " world " brought into
contrast with Jewish exclusivism ?   In fine, is not
the meaning of our text just this : that Jesus Christ
came to make propitiation for the sins not of Jews only,
but of the whole world, that is to say, not of course
for each and every man that lives in the world, but in
any event for men living throughout the world, heirs
of the world's life and partakers in the world's fortunes ? Certainly it is difficult for us to appreciate
the greatness of the revolution wrought in the religious
consciousness of men like John, bred in the exclusivism
of Judaism and accustomed to think of the Messiah as
the peculiar property of Israel, when the world-wide
mission of Christianity was brought home to their
minds and hearts. To John and men like John its
universalism was no doubt well-nigh the most astonishing fact about Christianity. And the declaration that
God so loved the world—not Israel merely, but the
world—that He gave His only begotten Son, that
whosoever—from every nation, not from the Jews
merely—should believe on Him should have eternal
life : this great declaration must have struck upon
their hearts with a revelation of the wideness of God's
mercy and the unfathomable profundities of His love,

such as we can scarcely appreciate in our days of age-long familiarity with the great fact. Is not this, then, the real meaning of the immense declaration of the text : that Jesus Christ is the world-wide Saviour, that now the middle-wall of partition has been broken down and God has called to Himself a people out of all the nations of the earth, and has so loved this His people gathered thus from the whole world, that He has given His only begotten Son to die for them ? And is not this a truth big with consequences, worthy of such a record as is given it in our text, and capable of awakening in our hearts a most profound response ?

Assuredly no one will doubt the value and inspiration of such suggestions. The truth that lies in them, who can gainsay ? But it is difficult to feel that they quite exhaust the meaning of the great words of the text. In their effort to do justice to the conception of the love of God, do they not do something less than justice to the conception embodied in the term " the world " ? In identifying " the world " with believers, do they not neglect, if we may not quite say the contrast of the two things, yet at least the distinction between the two notions which the text seems to institute ?   " God so loved the world," we read, " that He gave His only begotten Son, that whosoever believeth on Him should not perish, but have eternal

life." Certainly here " the world " and " believers "
do not seem to be quite equipollent terms : there
seems, surely, something conveyed by the one which
is not wholly taken up in the other. How, then, shall
we say that " the world " means just " the world of
believers," just those scattered through the world,
who, being the elect of God, shall believe in His Son
and so have eternal life ?   There is obviously much
truth in this idea : and the main difficulty which it
faces may, no doubt, be avoided by saying that what
is taught is that God's love of the world is shown by
His saving so great a multitude as He does save out
of the world. The wicked world deserved at His hands
only total destruction. But He saves out of it a multitude which no man can number, out of every nation,
and of all tribes and peoples and tongues. How much
must, then, God love the world ! This interpretation,
beyond question, reproduces the fundamental meaning
of the text. But does it completely satisfy all its
suggestions ?   Does there not lie in the text some
more subtle sequence of thought than is explicated by
it ? Is there not implied in it some profounder and
yet more glorious truth than even the world-wide reach
of God's love, manifested in the Great Commission,
and issuing in the multitude of the saved, the voice of
whose praise ascends to heaven as the voice of many
waters and as the voice of mighty thunders ?

Neither of the more common interpretations of the text, therefore, appears to bring out quite fully its real significance. The one fails to rise to the height of the conception of the love of God embodied in it ; the other appears to do something less than full justice to the conception of the world which God is said by it to love. The difficulty in both cases, seems to arise from a certain unwillingness to go deeply enough : a surface meaning, possible to impose upon the text, seems to be seized upon, while its profundities are left unexplored. If we would make our own the great revelation of the love of God here given us, we must be more patient. Renouncing the easy imposition upon it of meanings of our own devising, we must just permit the text to speak its own language to our hearts. Its prime intention is to convey some conception of the immeasurable greatness of the love of God. The method it employs to do this is to declare the love of God for the world so great that He gave His Son to save it. The central affirmation obviously, then, is this,—and it is a sufficiently great one to absorb our entire attention—that God loved the world. "God," "loved," "the world" —we must deal seriously with this great assertion, and with every element of it. We must first of all, then, thoroughly enter into the meaning of the three great terms here brought together : " God," " loved," " the world."

We shall not make the slightest step forward in understanding our text, for instance, so long as we permit ourselves to treat the great term " God " merely as the subject of a sentence. We must endeavour rather to rise as nearly as may be to its fullest significance. When we pronounce the word we must see to it that our minds are flooded with some wondering sense of God's infinitude, of His majesty, of His ineffable exaltation ; of His holiness, of His righteousness, of His flaming purity and stainless perfection. This is the Lord God Almighty whom the heaven of heavens cannot contain, to whom the earth is less than the small dust on the balance. He has no need of aught, nor can His unsullied blessedness be in any way affected—whether by way of increase or decrease —by any act of the creatures of His hands. What we call infinite space is but a speck on the horizon of His contemplation : what we call infinite time is in His sight but as yesterday when it is past. Serene in His unapproachable glory, His will is the resistless law of all existences to which their every motion conforms. Apparelled in majesty and girded with strength, righteousness and judgment are the foundations of His throne. He sits in the heavens and does whatsoever He pleases. It is this God, a God of whom to say that He is the Lord of all the earth is to say so little that it is to say nothing at all, of whom our text speaks.

And if we are ever to catch its meaning we must bear this fully in mind.

Now the text tells us of this God—of *this* God, remember,—that He loves. In itself, before we proceed a step further, this is a marvellous declaration. The metaphysicians have not yet plumbed it and still protest inability to construe the Absolute in terms of love. We shall not stop to dwell upon this somewhat abstract discussion. Enough for us that a God without emotional life would be a God without all that lends its highest dignity to personal spirit whose very being is movement ; and that is as much as to say no God at all. And more than enough for us that our text assures us that God loves, nay, that He is Love. What it concerns us now to note, however, is not the mere fact that He loves, but what it is that He is declared to love. For therein lies the climax of the great proclamation. This is nothing other than " the world." For this is the unimaginable declaration of the text : " God so loved the world." It is just in this that lies the mystery of the greatness of His love.

For what is this " world " which we are so strangely told that God loves ? We must not throw the reins on the neck of our fancy and seek a response that will suit our ideas of the right or the fitting. We must just let the Scriptures themselves tell us, and primarily that Apostle to whom we owe this great declaration.

Nor does he fail to tell us; and that without the slightest ambiguity. The "world," he tells us, is just the synonym of all that is evil and noisome and disgusting. There is nothing in it that can attract God's love,— nay, that can justify the love of any good man. It is a thing not to be dallied with, or acquiesced in : they that are of it, are by that very fact not of God ; and what the Christian has to do with it is just to overcome it ; for everything that is begotten of God manifests that great fact precisely by this—that he overcomes the world. "Love not the world, neither the things that are in the world," is John's insistent exhortation. And the reason for it he states very pungently : because "if any man love the world, the love of the Father is not in him." God and the world, then, are precise contradictions. "Nothing that is in the world is of the Father," we are told ; or, as it is put elsewhere in direct positive form : "The whole world lieth in the evil one." "The world, the flesh and the devil"—this is the pregnant combination in which we have learned from Scripture to express the baleful forces that war against the soul : and the three terms are thus cast together because they are essentially synonyms. See, then, whither we are brought. When we are told that God loves the world, it is much as if we were told that He loves the flesh and the devil. And we may, indeed, take courage from our text and

say it boldly : God does love the world and the flesh
and the devil. Therein indeed is the ground of all our
comfort and all our hope : for we—you and I—are
of the world and of the flesh and of the devil. Only,—
we must punctually note it,—the love wherewith God
loves the world, the flesh and the devil—therefore, us—
is not a love of complacency, as if He the Holy One
and the Good could take pleasure in what is worldly,
fleshly, devilish : but that love of benevolence which
would fain save us from our worldliness, fleshliness
and devilishness.

That indeed is precisely what the text goes on at
once to say : " For God so loved the world, that He
gave His only begotten Son, that whosoever believeth
on Him should not perish, but have eternal life." The
world then was perishing : and it was to save it that
God gave His Son. The text is, then, you see, in
principle an account of the coming of the Son of God
into the world. There were but two things for which
He, being what He was as the Son of God, could come
into the world, being what it was : to judge the world
or to save the world. It was for the latter that He
came. " For," the next verse runs on, " God sent not
His Son into the world to judge the world, but that
the world through Him should be saved." Not wrath,
then, though wrath were due, but love was the impelling cause of the coming of the Son of God into this

wicked world of ours. " For God so loved the world, that He gave His only begotten Son." The intensity of the love is what is emphasized : it was so intense that it was not deterred even by the sinfulness of its objects. You will perceive that what we have here then is, in effect, but the Johannean way of saying what Paul says when he tells us that " God commendeth His own love towards us, in that while we were yet sinners, Christ died for us." The marvel, in other words, which the text brings before us is just that marvel above all other marvels in this marvellous world of ours—the marvel of God's love for sinners. And this is the measure by which we are invited to measure the greatness of the love of God. It is not that it is so great that it is able to extend over the whole of a big world : it is so great that it is able to prevail over the Holy God's hatred and abhorrence of sin. For herein is love, that *God* could love the *world*—the world that lies in the evil one : that God who is all-holy and just and good, could so love this world that He gave His only begotten Son for it,—that He might not judge it, but that it might be saved.

The key to the passage lies, therefore, you see, in the significance of the term " world." It is not here a term of extension so much as a term of intensity. Its primary connotation is ethical, and the point of its employment is not to suggest that the world is so big that it takes a great deal of love to embrace it all, but that the world is so bad that it takes a great kind of love to love it at all, and much more to love it as God has loved it when He gave His Son for it. The whole debate as to whether the love here celebrated distributes itself to each and every man that enters into the composition of the world, or terminates on the elect alone chosen out of the world, lies thus outside the immediate scope of the passage and does not supply any key to its interpretation. The passage was not intended to teach, and certainly does not teach, that God loves all men alike and visits each and every one alike with the same manifestations of His love : and as little was it intended to teach or does it teach that His love is confined to a few especially chosen individuals selected out of the world. What it is intended to do is to arouse in our hearts a wondering sense of the marvel and the mystery of the love of God for the sinful world—conceived, here, not quantitatively but qualitatively as, in its very distinguishing characteristic, sinful. And search the universe through and through—in all its recesses and through all its historical development—and you will find no marvel so great, no mystery so unfathomable, as this, that the great and good God, whose perfect righteousness flames in indignation at the sight of every iniquity and whose absolute holiness recoils in abhorrence in the

presence of every impurity, yet loves this sinful world,
—yes, has so loved it that He has given His only begotten Son to die for it. It is this marvel and this
mystery that our text would fain carry home to our
hearts, and we would be wise if we would permit them
to be absorbed in its contemplation.

At the same time, however, although we cannot
permit the passage to be interpreted in the terms of
the debate in question, it would not be quite true to
say it has no bearing upon that debate.

One thing, for instance, which the passage tells us,
and tells us with great emphasis, is that the love which
it celebrates is a saving love ; not a love which merely
tends towards salvation, and may—perhaps easily—
be defeated in its aim by, say, the unwillingness of its
objects. The very point of the passage lies, on the one
side, in the mightiness of the love of God ; and on the
other in the unwillingness not of some but of all its
objects. The love here celebrated is, we must remember, the love of *God*—of the Lord God Almighty :
and it is love to the *world*—which altogether " lies in
the evil one." It is a love which is great, and powerful,
and all-conquering ; which attains its end, and will
not stand helpless before any obstacle. It is the precise
purpose of the passage to teach us this, to raise our
hearts to some apprehension of the inconceivable
greatness of the love of God, set as it is upon saving

the wicked world. It would be possible to believe that such a love as this terminates equally and with the same intent upon each and every man who is in " the world," only if we may at the same time believe that it works out its end completely and with full effect on each and every man. But this the passage explicitly forbids us to believe, proceeding at once to divide the " world " into two classes, those that perish and those that have eternal life. The almighty, all-conquering love of God, therefore, certainly does not pour itself equally and with the same intent upon each and every man in the world. In the sovereignty that belongs of necessity to His love as to all love, He rather visits with it whom He will.

But neither will the text allow us to suppose that God grants this His immeasurable love only to a few, abstracted from the world, while the world itself He permits to fall away to its destruction. The declaration is, not that God has loved some out of the world, but that He has loved the world. And we must rise to the height of this divine universalism. It is the world that God has loved with His deathless love, this sinful world of ours : and it is the world, this sinful world of ours, that He has given His Son to die for : and it is the world that through the sacrifice of His dear Son, He has saved, this very sinful world of ours. " God sent not His Son into the world," we read,

" to judge the world, but that the world should be saved by Him " : that is to say, God did not send His Son into the world for the purpose of judging the world, but for the purpose of saving the world : a declaration which could not be true if, despite His coming, the world were lost and only a select few saved out of it. The purposes of God do not fail.

You must not fancy, then, that God sits helplessly by while the world, which He has created for Himself, hurtles hopelessly to destruction, and He is able only to snatch with difficulty here and there a brand from the universal burning. The world does not govern Him in a single one of His acts : He governs it and leads it steadily onward to the end which, from the beginning, or ever a beam of it had been laid, He had determined for it. As it was created for His glory, so shall it show forth His praise : and this human race on which He has impressed His image shall reflect that image in the beauty of the holiness which is its supreme trait. The elect—they are not the residuum of the great conflagration, the ashes, so to speak, of the burnt-up world, gathered sadly together by the Creator, after the catastrophe is over, that He may make a new and perhaps better beginning with them and build from them, perchance, a new structure, to replace that which has been lost. Nay, they are themselves " the world " ; not the world as it is in its

sin, lying in the evil one ; but the world in its promise
and potency of renewed life. Through all the years
one increasing purpose runs, one *increasing* purpose :
the kingdoms of the earth become ever more and
more the kingdom of our God and His Christ. The
process may be slow ; the progress may appear to our
impatient eyes to lag. But it is God who is building :
and under His hands the structure rises as steadily
as it does slowly, and in due time the capstone shall
be set into its place, and to our astonished eyes shall
be revealed nothing less than a saved world.

Meanwhile, we who live in the midst of the process
see not yet the end. These are days of incomplete-
ness, and it is only by faith that we can perceive the
issue. The kingdom of God is as yet only in the making;
and the " world " is not yet saved. So, there appear
about us two classes : there are those that perish as
well as those that have eternal life. With the absoluteness which characterizes the writer of this Gospel,
these two classes are set before us in the text and in
the paragraph of which it forms a part, in their intrinsic
antagonism. They are believers and unbelievers in
the Son of God : and they are believers and unbelievers in the Son of God, because they are in their
essential natures good or bad, lovers of light or lovers
of darkness. " For every one that doeth evil hateth
the light and cometh not to the light ; but he that

doeth the truth cometh to the light." Throughout the whole process of the world's development, therefore, the Light that has come into the world draws to Itself those that are of the light : He, that is, who through love of the world came into the world to save the world,—yea, and who shall save the world—in the meantime attaches to Himself in every generation those who in their essential nature belong to Him. How they come to be His, and therefore to be attracted to Him, and therefore to enter into the life that is life indeed—to become portions no longer of the world that lies in the evil one, but of the reconstructed world that abides in Him—the paragraph in which our text is set leaves us much uninformed. Accordingly some rash expositors wish to insist that to it the division of men into the essentially good and the essentially bad is an ultimate fact. They speak therefore much of the ineradicable dualism of Jesus' conception, not staying to consider the confusion thus wrought in the whole paragraph. For in that case how could there be talk of the Son of God coming into the world to *save* the world ? Obviously, to the text, those that belong to the Son themselves require saving ; that is to say, no less than the lost themselves, they belong by nature to the " evil one," in whom the whole world—not a part of it only—we are told explicitly " lieth."

And if we will but attend to the context in which our paragraph is set, we will perceive that we are not left without guidance to its proper understanding. For we must remember that this paragraph is not an isolated document standing off to itself and complete in itself, but is a comment upon the discourse of our Lord to Nicodemus. It necessarily receives its colour and explanation, therefore, from that discourse of which it is either a substantive part or upon which it is at least a reflection. And what does that discourse teach us except this : that all that is born of flesh is flesh, and only what is reborn of Spirit is Spirit ; that no man can enter the Kingdom of God, therefore, except he be born again of God ; and that this birth is not at the command of men, but is the gift of a Spirit which is like the wind that bloweth where it listeth, the sound whereof we hear though we know not whence it cometh and whither it goeth—but can say of it only, Lo, it is here ! Here then is the explanation of the essential difference in men revealed in the varying reception they give to the Son of God. It is not due to accident of birth or to diversity of experience in the world, least of all to inherent qualities of goodness or badness belonging to each by nature. It is due solely to this,—whether or not they have been born again by the Spirit and so are of the light and come spontaneously to the light when it dawns upon their waiting eyes. The sequence in this great process of salvation, then, according to our passage, when taken in its context, is this : the gift of the Son of God to save the world ; the preparation of the hearts of men to receive the Son of God in vital faith : the attraction of these " children of the light " to the Light of the world ; and the gradual rebuilding of the fabric of the world along the lines of God's choosing into that kingdom of light which is thus progressively prepared for its perfect revelation at the last day.

Thus, thus, then, it is that God is saving the world —the world, mind you, and not merely some individuals out of the world : by a process which involves not supplanting but reformation, recreation. We look for new heavens and a new earth, it is true ; but these new heavens and new earth are not another heaven and another earth, but the old heaven and old earth renewed ; or as the Scriptures phrase it " regenerated." For not the individual merely but the world-fabric itself is to be regenerated in that " regeneration when the Son of Man is to sit on the throne of His glory." During the process there may be much that is discarded : but when the process is completed, then also shall be completed the task which the Son of Man has taken upon Himself, and the " world " shall be saved—this wicked world of sinful men transformed into a world of righteousness.

Surely, we shall not wish to measure the saving work of God by what has been already accomplished in these unripe days in which our lot is cast. The sands of time have not yet run out. And before us stretch, not merely the reaches of the ages, but the infinitely resourceful reaches of the promise of God. Are not the saints to inherit the earth ? Is not the recreated earth theirs ? Are not the kingdoms of the world to become the Kingdom of God ? Is not the knowledge of the glory of God to cover the earth as the waters cover the sea ? Shall not the day dawn when no man need say to his neighbour, " Know the Lord," for all shall know Him from the least unto the greatest ? O raise your eyes, raise your eyes, I beseech you, to the far horizon : let them rest nowhere short of the extreme limit of the divine purpose of grace. And tell me what you see there. Is it not the supreme, the glorious, issue of that love of God which loved, not one here and there only in the world, but the world in its organic completeness ; and gave His Son, not to judge the world, but that the world through Him should be saved ? And He said unto me, " Come hither, I will shew thee the bride, the wife of the Lamb. And he . . . shewed me the holy city Jerusalem, coming down out of heaven from God, having the glory of God. . . . And the city hath no need of the sun, neither of the moon, to shine upon it : for

K

the glory of God did lighten it, and the Lamb, the lamp thereof. And the nations shall walk amidst the light thereof ; and the kings of the earth do bring their glory into it. And the gates thereof shall in no wise be shut by day (for there shall be no night there) : and they shall bring the glory and the honour of the nations into it : and there shall in no wise enter into it anything unclean, or he that maketh an abomination and a lie ; but only they which are written in the Lamb's book of life." Only those written in the Lamb's book of life, and yet all the nations ! It is the vision of the saved world. "For God so loved the world, that He gave His only begotten Son, that whosoever believeth in Him should not perish, but have eternal life." It is the vision of the consummated purpose of the immeasurable love of God.

THE GOSPEL OF PAUL

2 CORINTHIANS v. 14–15, 18–19, 21 :—For the love of Christ constraineth us ; because we thus judge, that one died for all, therefore all died ; and He died for all, that they which live should no longer live unto themselves, but unto Him who for their sakes died and rose again. . . . But all things are of God, who reconciled us to Himself through Christ, and gave unto us the ministry of reconciliation ; to wit, that God was in Christ reconciling the world unto Himself, not reckoning unto them their trespasses. . . . Him who knew no sin He made to be sin on our behalf ; that we might become the righteousness of God in Him.

THE GOSPEL OF PAUL

I HAVE chosen for my text three sentences which do not form a consecutive passage. They stand, however, in very close contiguity within the limits of a single short paragraph, within the narrow compass, indeed, of eight verses. More than that, they stand out upon the face of this short paragraph as marked features, from which it receives its character and chief significance. Glancing over this paragraph, the eye can no more fail to fix itself upon these three sentences than gazing over a rich plain from some high point of sight it could fail to be attracted by a series of bold promontories throwing themselves athwart it ; or glancing on the fretted lid of some highly wrought casket it could fail to be drawn and dazzled by the jewels which blaze upon it. We cannot say, indeed, that the paragraph exists for these three sentences : they, rather, are here for the purposes of the paragraph and fulfil these purposes with perfection. But in prosecuting the end he has here in view the apostle is led to make his appeal to considerations of so high an order that the sentences in which they are adduced stand out above the general drift of the discussion like mountain-peaks in a plain, glow on its surface like jewels in their setting.

What Paul is engaged upon in this section of his Epistle is the vindication of his integrity as a minister of grace, and of the purity of the Gospel he preached. It is in full view of the judgment-seat of Christ, he asserts, that he prosecutes the mission that has been committed to him ; and he has permitted nothing to deflect him by a hair's-breadth from the message which has been placed on his lips. In giving force to this contention he is led to enunciate the contents of the message of which he has been made the bearer : and it is this enunciation which is thrown up to our view in these sentences I have chosen for my text.

In these sentences is contained therefore the announcement of Paul's Gospel ; and it is this fact which gives them their distinction. Search throughout the whole compass of Paul's Epistles and it is doubtful if you will find another such succinct, complete and pungent statement of the Gospel which Paul preached ; of what he deemed the very touchstone and heart of the message he brought to men. Certainly you will find none more formally set forth as the apostle's own declaration of the essence of his Gospel. If we wish to know precisely what Paul preached and precisely in what he conceived all that he preached to centre and to be summed up, we cannot do better than attend to these crisp sentences.

I have called them crisp sentences, and I might

almost have spoken of them as detached sentences.
For part and parcel as they are of Paul's argument,
fitting into it and bearing their part in it with the
perfection of sentences born of the discussion of the
moment, they yet have an odd air of detachment
about them, which seems to assure us they were not
struck out in the heat of this debate, but have been
brought into it from without. One of them is introduced by what we may almost call a formula of
citation : " because we thus judge "—" seeing that
our judgment is this,"—viz. what follows. All of
them are phrased with that sharply cut frugality of
language which belongs to proverbial speech, and is
the result, no doubt, of the attrition which sentences
suffer from much repetition, by which all the rough
edges, like superfluous particles, are worn off. " One
died for all : therefore all died : and He died for all
that, living, they might no longer live to themselves,
but to Him who died and rose for them." " All is of
God ; who reconciled us with Himself through Christ
and gave us the ministry of reconciliation, since it
was God who in Christ was reconciling the world with
Himself." " Him that knew no sin He made sin for
us, that we might become the righteousness of God in
Him." There is not a redundant word in any of these
sentences ; there is even a notable parsimony of
words ; even what might have been deemed the

necessary connecting particles are omitted. I think we may be quite sure that these sentences were not first framed as Paul set them down on the sheets of this letter ; that they had often been on his lips before ; and that they went down on the sheets he was writing here in the form they had taken on his lips after numerous repetitions. In a word, we have here the phrases in which Paul was accustomed to give expression to the heart of his Gospel.

It is tempting to turn aside to remark upon the analogy supplied by this discovery to a phenomenon characteristic of the so-called Pastoral Epistles, in which we repeatedly meet with gnome-like announcements of the great truths of the Gospel, encysted, as it were, in the tissues of the Epistle. It would seem that from the beginning Paul was accustomed to imbed in his Epistles the " faithful sayings " in which he was wont to find adequate expression given to the mighty truths it was his life-work to make effective among men. It is important, however, that we should not permit our attention to be distracted from the main point which now claims it. This is that we have in the sentences now before us not only an announcement of the essence of Paul's Gospel, perhaps the most clear and formal announcement of its essence to be found in his Epistles, but also this announcement in the form which he habitually gave it. It was in these precise words that Paul was accustomed to express himself when he desired to carry the essence of his Gospel home to the minds of men and fix it there with precision and in unmistakable and unalterable distinctness. We may approach the study of these sentences, then, with the utmost confidence that we have in them not some chance, perhaps one-sided, deliverance valid only for the immediate purpose of a particular controversy, but the well-weighed and carefully compacted expression of the very core of his Gospel, that Gospel which had been committed to him by the Lord Himself, by which he won the world, upon which he nourished his own spirit, and which he offers to us as the very word of life.

What, then, is this Gospel of Paul, brought before us here with such directness and energy of expression?

Casting our eye over the sentences in which it is embodied, we are struck at once with the fact that it is a universalistic Gospel. We should have expected this of Paul. The hinge upon which his whole life-work turned was the universalizing of the Gospel of Christ. It was therefore that he was the Apostle of the Gentiles. And it was out of this that all his conflicts, trials, sufferings arose. The bitter strife in which he was engaged in this very Church of Corinth, one campaign of which is fought out in this letter, was itself rooted in the universalism of his Gospel. It could not be that the note of this universalism should be unheard in anything that can put in the slightest claim to be the embodiment of Paul's Gospel.

It is so little unheard here that it would be truer to say that it forms the ground-tone of the whole enunciation. " One died for all : therefore all died "— that is the key-note which is struck at the beginning. " God was in Christ reconciling the world with Himself "—that is the great announcement in which it culminates. We may be perfectly sure that neither statement was here made by Paul for the first time. Rather, these were the things on which he had fed his courage in those days of afflictions, necessities, distresses, stripes, imprisonments, tumults, labours, watchings, fastings, in which his life had been spent. We may fancy him in the midst of the deaths which he died daily repeating to himself over and over again these great words : " One died for all : therefore all died " : " God was in Christ reconciling the world with Himself "—and deriving from them the force by virtue of which, though he died yet behold he lived again, though he was chastened yet he was not destroyed, though he was brought to grief yet he always rejoiced, though he was himself poor he yet enriched many, though he had nothing he yet possessed all things. They constitute indeed the battle-cry of Paul's whole immense conflict and give its character to his entire life-history. Eliminate this note of universalism from Paul's Gospel and you do away with his significance in history ; you cut up the Gospel to which he freely gave his life by the roots.

You cannot exaggerate, therefore, the significance to his Gospel of Paul's universalism. In important respects this universalism was his Gospel. But unfortunately it is very possible to misconceive and to misrepresent this universalism : and unhappily it is commonly very gravely misconceived and mis-represented. After all, Paul's universalism was *Paul's* universalism ; and *Paul's* universalism stood in op-position, not to the particularism of divine grace, but to the exclusiveness of Jewish nationalism. What he gave his life to, what he directed all his teaching toward, was not a passionate assertion of absolute indiscrimination on God's part in His dealings with sinners of the human race, but the vindication to the Gospel of God's grace in Christ Jesus of a world-wide reference. If he argues at one time that " there is no difference " between men, he makes it plain that he means this in point of claim upon God for His mercy ; and so soon as he comes to speak of the distribution of the divine gifts, he makes it equally plain that there is a great difference and that this difference depends on the will of the Divine Giver. When Paul therefore

nailed to his mast-head the great declaration : " One
died for all ; therefore all died," he was as far as
possible from intimating that Jesus' death was equally
and without distinction in behalf of every individual
of the human race, and that therefore every individual
of the human race, past, present and to come, died
with Christ on the cross. This crass distributive
universalism of redemption apparently never once
entered his mind. And equally, when he inscribed
upon his banner, " God was in Christ reconciling the
world with Himself," he thought of nothing so little
as teaching that this reconciliation concerned itself
equally with each and every individual who has ever
lived in the world, lives in it now, or ever shall live in
it. Such a conception is quite alien to his entire
thought. What he means is just that God, who is
the God not of the Jews only but also of the Gentiles,
has given His Son to die not for the Jews only but
for the world. His eye has caught this great vision ;
and, his mouth being open and his heart enlarged, he
cries, Not one people only, but the world for Christ !
It is the great missionary cry which Paul gives us
here. " The world for Christ ! " That is the cry that
sounds in our ears to-day and fills us with enthusiasm
in our service of the cross. It is the cry which Paul
heard in his heart two thousand years ago, and under
the impulse of which he inaugurated that great

mission work which still occupies our hearts and hands. " The world for Christ "—not one nation, not one class, not one race or condition of men, but the world and nothing less than the world for Christ !

It would certainly be exceedingly unfortunate in any event to eviscerate Paul's whole Gospel for the sake of gratuitously imposing on his language an inoperative universalism of redemption which does not actually save. That men could perish for whom Christ died, Paul never imagined that human minds could conceive. The very nerve of his great declaration that " Christ died for all ; therefore all died," is that participation in the death of Christ is salvation. Therefore he goes on to declare that those who thus die with Christ live, live with the Christ who not only died for them but also rose again for them. So little was it possible for him to admit a distinction between dying with Christ, which is the unconscious lot of all, and living with Christ, which is the conscious attainment of only some, that he even founds elsewhere an *a fortiori* argument on participation in Christ's death as removing all doubt of participation in His life. " But God commendeth His own Son towards us," he reasons, " in that while we were yet sinners Christ died for us. Much more then, being now justified by His blood, shall we be saved from wrath through Him. For if while we were sinners, we were reconciled with God through the death of His Son, much more, being reconciled, shall we be saved by His life." " But if we died with Christ," he reasons again, " we believe that we shall also live with Him " ; and again, " For if we have become united with Him by the likeness of His death, we shall be also by the likeness of His resurrection." Paul therefore will have nothing to do with a distinction between men who have only died with Christ and those who also live with Him. With Paul, to die with Christ means to live together with Him ; to be reconciled with God through the death of Christ means to enter into the full inheritance of life. When he passionately declares that when Christ died He died not for Jews only but for all, that in Him God was reconciling nothing less than the world with Himself, he is thinking of no half-measures. He is proclaiming the world-wide reach, the world-wide destiny of God's salvation.

How impossible it is to read Paul as teaching here a purely potential universalism in the death of Christ, to be made effective in each instance by the individual's own act of appropriation, is rendered clear by another prime characteristic of his Gospel as here enunciated. This is what we may perhaps call, for lack of a better phrase, its high supernaturalism. By this we mean to refer to the emphasis and persistence with which he ascribes the whole saving process—in its initiation and outworking alike—to God. This too we should have expected of Paul. There is no more marked feature of his total thought than the vision of God which informs it : and no matter from what point of departure his argument takes its start, it can find its point of rest only when it arrives at " the good pleasure of His will, to the praise of the glory of His grace, which He freely bestowed on us in the Beloved." It can cause us no surprise therefore when we find him in our present passage insisting, of the new life which he discovers in those—in all those—who have died with Christ, that it is all of God ; and representing the whole tremendous transaction by which we sinners are transformed into the likeness of Christ as inaugurated and carried through by God alone. All those for whom Christ died He tells us died with Him and rose again with Him, and are consequently a new creation, the old things having passed away and become new. And then he adds with what might almost seem superfluous emphasis—for how could these things be, except by the power of God ?—" But all these things are of God, who it is that has reconciled us with Himself through Christ and has given to us the ministry of reconciliation, seeing that it was God " (observe the emphasis again) " who in Christ was reconciling the world with Himself." Accordingly, when a few verses later he alludes to the redemptive

process again, he tells us quite naturally, not that
" He who knew no sin was made sin for us," but that
" Him who knew no sin God made sin for us, that we
might become the righteousness of God in Him." So
eager is the apostle that his readers shall take off
from his page at least this assurance, that what they
are in Christ Jesus and all that they shall become
they owe to God and to God alone. It was He, he
tells us, who made Christ, the sinless one, to be sin for
us ; it was He who reconciled us with Himself through
Christ ; it is of Him that we are new creatures in
Christ. In the whole saving process we supply nothing
but the sinners to be saved, and the consequent
activities induced in us by the saving process, as, in
accordance with our nature, we move as we are
moved upon.

It surely belongs to the most astonishing curiosities
of exposition, then, that in the face of this abounding
emphasis upon the sole efficiency of God in salvation,
there should be found those who insist that, according
to Paul's teaching, the decisive act in salvation is
supplied by an action of the human will. See, we are
told, the apostle in this very context beseeches his
readers not to permit the grace of God to come to them
in vain, but to be reconciled with God. Does not this
imply that all that God has done lies without us, and
it belongs to us, in our sovereign freedom, to give it

validity each for his own person ? We need not pause
to point out that the inference thus so confidently
drawn is explicitly contradicted a score of times elsewhere by the apostle, who consistently represents it as
" of God " that men differ in their spiritual endowments;
and declares that no one has the least advantage over
another which he has not received from above, and
therefore cannot glory in it as if it were of his own
production,—that, in a word, in the matter of spiritual
standing, it is not of him that willeth nor of him that
runneth but of God that showeth mercy. Nor need
we pause to point out that there is a great difference,
which we dare not neglect in a matter like the present,
between an exhortation to action in accordance with
the really moving force, and exhortation to action
designed to set this force in motion. When this same
apostle exhorts us to work out our own salvation with
fear and trembling, "for it is God who is working in you
both the willing and the doing for His good pleasure,"
we certainly cannot infer that our salvation so hangs
upon our own will that God's energizing waits upon
our act : the contrary is openly asserted—that our
act rests rather on His energizing ; it is He that works
our very willing as well as our doing. Similarly it can
scarcely be inferred from Paul's exhortation to us " to
be reconciled with God," that reconciliation with God
so depends on the unmoved action of our own free-

L

will that all of God's action looking to our salvation must wait upon it. Apart from all this, it would seem to be enough to observe that no inference of this kind can set aside Paul's explicit and emphatic ascription here of this very reconciliation to God. For it is precisely our reconciliation which Paul ascribes to God with what seems almost an excessive energy of emphasis : " All these things are of God, who it was that reconciled us with Himself through Jesus Christ " : " It was God who, in Christ, was reconciling the world with Himself." When, immediately after this strong assertion of the divine production of reconciliation, he entreats his readers to be reconciled with God, the one most certain thing of all is that he does not mean to imply that their reconciliation is so in their own hands that the act of God waits upon their act. And this becomes the more evident when we observe that even in this exhortation itself the verb is thrown into the passive voice, and points therefore not to something which we are to do, but to something which we are to suffer. The exhortation, in other words, is not that we should " reconcile ourselves " to God, but that we should assume an attitude consonant with the reconciliation which God has wrought with respect to us. That is to say, we have a conception here which ranges perfectly with that other exhortation which we have already illustratively adduced : that we should work out our own salvation, knowing it is God who is working in us both the willing and the doing. It is an exhortation to consonant, not to determining activity.

We are led thus, however, to advert to a further prime characteristic of the Gospel of Paul, as set forth in our passage. That is, that it finds its key-note in a doctrine of reconciliation. The core of Paul's Gospel is indeed expressed in this one word, Reconciliation; and it behoves us to consider carefully what he means by it. There are several things that are told us about it in our present passage. In the first place we are very emphatically told, as we have just seen, that the author of it is God: it is God Himself, not man, who works this reconciliation. "All these things," says the apostle, "are of God, who it is that has reconciled us with Himself through Christ." "For it was God who in Christ was reconciling the world with Himself." Next we are told that the effects by which this reconciliation manifests itself among men are relief from the burden of their sin, and the proclamation of free pardon. "It was surely God who in Christ was reconciling the world with Himself, since He does not impute to them their trespasses and has placed in us the word of reconciliation." Then we are told that it finds its ground in the sin-bearing of Christ. "We beseech you in the

behalf of Christ, Be ye reconciled with God : Him
who knew no sin He made sin for us, that we may
be the righteousness of God in Him." From such
suggestions as these it is perfectly easy to see what
Paul means by this reconciliation, the ministry of
which he declares to be his only function, the proclamation of which his one duty—or rather privilege—in
the world. It is, shortly, not the reconciliation of man
to God, as the shortcomings of our English version
might mislead us into supposing : but the reconciliation
of God to man—a reconciliation which God has Himself
undertaken and which He has accomplished at the
tremendous cost of the death of His Son, on the ground
of which He is able to release men from their trespasses. Of course men are at enmity with God : they
do not like even to retain God in their knowledge, and
they turn against Him with unconcealed dread and
hatred. But this is not the thing which most disturbs
Paul. What most disturbs him is that God is at
enmity with man : that His wrath is revealed from
heaven against their abounding unrighteousness. And
what fills his heart with joy—the joy that made him
the zealous missionary he was,—is the assurance that
this enmity has been removed, that this wrath has
been appeased and that by God Himself, who has
reconciled us with Himself through Christ, by making
Him who knew no sin to be sin for us,—and so enabling

Himself not to impute our trespasses to us. The proclamation of this great transaction seemed to Paul so
glorious that he joyfully made the ministry of reconciliation his life-work; the word of reconciliation his Gospel.
In it lies, in a word, the very heart of Paul's Gospel.

Now the presupposition of this Gospel, you will
perceive, is a deep and keen sense of human sin and
that in the aspect of guilt. The reason why Paul's
heart was filled with such joy at the thought of a
reconciled God was that his heart was oppressed with
a sense of guilt in the presence of a just God. A holy
and righteous God, he knew, could not possibly look
upon him, or his partners in guilt, without abhorrence
and indignation. In his conscience the wrath of God
was revealed against the abounding iniquity of men.
O wretched men that we are, his soul of souls cried
out, who shall deliver us from this mass of sin? It
was because he felt so deeply and keenly the guilt of
sin, and knew so clearly the depth and heinousness of
his own and of the world's guilt, that he broke out with
such rejoicing at the sight of a reconciled God, and
made the proclamation of His reconciliation his
Gospel—the substance of the glad tidings which he
bore to a sin-stricken and hopeless race. The underlying conception of sin,—of sin oppressing, of sin
removed—thus dominates the passages which are now
engaging our attention. Why should Christ,—the

" One "—need to die for men : and why is it glad
tidings that all for whom He died, died with Him ?
Why should the Gospel of reconciliation be announced
as manifesting itself precisely in the non-imputation
of men's trespasses to them ?   Why above all should
the exhortation to be reconciled with God be supported
by the great declaration that He who knew no sin has
been made sin for us ?   Is it not clear that underneath
all Paul's Gospel lies the most profound and poignant
sense of sin, and that his Gospel consists precisely in a
proclamation of relief from the intolerable burden of
guilt ?   This then was the word of reconciliation, the
ministry of which was committed to him : that the
righteous wrath of God against sin has been appeased
and the face of God has been turned to us again
clothed in a smile of favour.

It has seemed worth while to dwell upon this,
partly because of the apparent dying out of a deep
sense of sin in wide circles of present-day life, but
more because this sense of sin though it may be
temporarily obscured cannot really die out, but will
sooner or later assert itself in every human breast and
bring despair when it does not find its antidote in a
sense of a reconciled God.   No doubt our age is marked
by a " vanishing sense of sin," and there are multitudes
about us who seem never to have awakened to any
adequate realization of their moral condition, or of

the significance of their moral condition with respect
to their relations to God and to that future over which
the righteous award of God rules. It would not be
strange if there were some sitting here to-day to whom
Paul's strong agony under the consciousness of sin
seems wholly alien to normal human experience,
something at any rate into which they find it impossible
sympathetically to enter. I do not say that this
condition of apathy in face of the most tremendous
fact of human life is scarcely creditable to you : I do
not even say that it ought to be viewed by you as a
signal of extreme danger, because it is the index of an
indurated heart, a heart callous to its own wickedness,
and therefore should cause you the deepest concern
and call out your best endeavours to see things more
truly even if less comfortably. What I wish to say
now to you is, that it is a condition that cannot last.
We are all sinners : and, being sinners, we are under
the condemnation of the just God, who does righteousness in heaven and on earth. We cannot always
conceal from ourselves this state of things. Sooner or
later our troubled eyes will open with fright upon it :
and all our smug contentment with ourselves will be
gone. Now, life may run on upon oiled axles. Then,
Time will seem to us " a maniac scattering dust, and
Life a Fury slinging flame.'' And then, having discovered what sin is and what we are as sinners, we

shall discover also the joy which Paul felt at the vision of a reconciled God. It will no longer seem strange to us that our Lord declared that there is joy in heaven over one sinner that repents, more than over ninety and nine just persons who need no repentance. It will no longer be difficult for us to understand that the gladdest of all glad tidings which the apostle knew to bring to the world, was the glad tidings of reconciliation in the blood of Jesus Christ.

I say, reconciliation in the blood of Jesus Christ. For we do not get to the heart of Paul's doctrine of reconciliation, until we bring clearly before us what he teaches us of the way in which it has been accomplished. That way is, briefly, by a great act of substitution : of the substitution of Jesus Christ for us before the judgment-seat of God and the expiating of our guilt by Him on the tree. If Paul's doctrine of reconciliation is the heart of his Gospel, his doctrine of substitution is the heart of the heart of his Gospel. In it all the glad tidings he had to proclaim to man culminate and find their true significance. What does Paul mean by that great declaration which stands in the forefront of our present passage : " One died for all : therefore all died " ? And what does he mean by that even greater declaration with which the passage closes : " Him who knew no sin God made sin for us " ? Obviously what he means is just substi-

tution. We must not lose ourselves here in possibly
learned but certainly meaningless discussions of the
precise fundamental significance of the preposition
" for."   Of course its fundamental meaning is " for
the sake of," " for the benefit of."   It was for the sake
of the all that Christ died ; and it was precisely
because He died for their sakes that they share in
that death of His which was for *their* benefit and not
for *His*.   It was for our sakes that God made Him who
knew no sin to be sin ; and it is precisely because this
great transaction was done for our benefit that it
avails for us.   And what else could Paul have meant
when he cries out in the joy of his salvation, " Christ
died for me," " God made Him sin for me," than just
that Christ had died for his sake and it inured to his
benefit that He had been made sin ?   Would you
expect a beneficiary of this tremendous transaction,
suffused with a sense of the immense benefit received,
to employ in describing it language which was wholly
denuded of all emotional recognition that it was all
for him, for his sake ?   And this is the real account to
give of the prevalence in the allusions of the Biblical
writers to the death of Christ of the broad preposition
" for," with the primary implication of " for the sake
of," rather than of the more precise " for " with the
primary implication of " instead of," in relating that
death to themselves.   They were not putting together

a systematic statement of the exact relation of Christ's death to human salvation : they were giving expression to their deepest religious convictions, and they could not but choose language charged with their profound emotions. When they employ the particular preposition they do employ, they derogate nothing from the substitutive nature of the death they are describing, but they couch their description of it in language freighted with their answering gratitude and love. When Paul declares that when Christ died in behalf of all, then all died with Him—that God made Him sin in our behalf though He Himself knew no sin—he asserts substitution just as clearly as if he had said that He died in our stead and had been made sin in our place ; and at the same time he uncovers to us his own heart, throbbing with grateful response to such an unheard-of benefit.

The glad tidings which Paul's Gospel brings to men, then, is just, to put it briefly and in familiar language, salvation from sin in the blood of Jesus Christ. What it means is, in the crispest form of statement, just that Jesus has done it all. He has taken our place and borne in His own body on the tree all our iniquities : He has died our death : and He grants us His righteousness that hereafter we may live and live to Him. This, according to Paul, is the very heart of the heart of the Gospel.

And now let us observe finally what according to Paul is the issue of all this for life. Here we have brought before us yet another primary characteristic of his Gospel. Shall we say, Because Jesus has done it all, there remains nothing for us to do? So says not Paul. We could not save ourselves, or do the least thing towards, or contributing to, our salvation. Until Jesus had died for us there was nothing for us to do but to die. We were dead in sin, and held under death for sin. But now since He has died for us, we can work our salvation out into life. And that is what Paul teaches us. We cannot save ourselves: but having been saved, we can illustrate our salvation in newness of life. " One died for all," he says, " therefore all died : and He died for all, that, living, they might no longer live for themselves, but to Him who for them died and rose again." " He that knew no sin was made sin for us, that we might become the righteousness of God in Him." " So then, if anyone is in Christ, he is a new creature : the old things have passed away, behold, they have become new." There is, it will be observed, a declaration here and an exhortation. The declaration is that this newness of life is the result of salvation in Christ. The exhortation is that we shall walk in accordance with this newness of life. The apostle does not leave it an open question whether those for whom Christ has died (and who, therefore,—so he says—have died with Him) shall possess this new life. He says they *are* " a new creation " ; and a new *creation* is not a self-made thing, which waits upon our own choice whether it is made or not ; but a product of the almighty power of God. And therefore the apostle at once adds that it has God for its author : " And all these things are of God." If Christ died for us, He died for us only for this end—that we may live and, living, may live not for ourselves, but to Him. If He was made sin for us, He was made sin for us only for this end—that we may be the righteousness of God in Him. The end can no more fail than the means. He who is in Christ Jesus is a " new creation." To him the old things have passed away ; all has become wholly new. Paul had found it so : and he makes his finding it so the substance of his defence to the Corinthians. He could not but be true to his mission and office as an apostle of Christ : for it was the love of Christ—not *his* love *to Christ*, but *Christ's* love *to him*—which constrained him—held him in—that he should not give himself to aught but that to which he was sent. Being in Christ, he was a new creation, and everything that was of the flesh had fallen away from him.

And every one who, like Paul, has been made the object of Christ's love, for whom Christ has died, and who has been made partaker of Christ's death, will like Paul find the love of Christ constraining him, will find the life of Christ flowing into his veins, will discover himself a new creation, looking out as such on a new world, filled with new enthusiasms, directing himself to new ends. You cannot die with Christ and not rise again with Him : it cannot be that He who knew no sin shall have been made sin for you, and you who have known no righteousness shall not be made the righteousness of God in Him. This is Paul's declaration to you : and there could be no declaration of greater joy. Being in Christ Jesus, you have within you the powers of a new life, and they will grow, and grow, and grow. Sinner that you are, Christ who knew no sin has been made sin for you, and you shall become the righteousness of God in Him. Could there be a greater inducement to effort brought to bear upon us than this great declaration ? It is God that is working in us : shall we not then work out our own salvation with fear and trembling ? This is Paul's exhortation to you. In effect he says : Seeing that you are a new creation, live as becomes those who are a new creation. Desert the old plane of your living ; it is not worthy of new creatures. Having died with Christ, live with and for Him. He has been made sin for you. See that you become the righteousness of God in Him. You are released from the bondage of sin and freed for a new life of holiness. Live it. Adorn the

Gospel you profess : for God has called you not to sin but to holiness, and if you walk not in this holiness,— are you in Him ? have you died with Him ? He who dies with Him lives also in and with Him, and living in and with Him lives to Him.

So the apostle mingles declaration and exhortation, warning and encouragement ; and the upshot of it all is, as we cannot have failed long ere this to have told ourselves, that the Gospel he preaches is an eminently ethical Gospel. Righteousness in Christ, righteousness through Christ,—justification, sanctification—these things do not stand with the apostle as separable entities over against one another, one of which can be had without the other. They are distinctly correlatives, implying and implicating one the other. It would be inconceivable to him that there could be sanctification which did not rest on justification, or that there could be justification which did not issue in sanctification. To die with Christ is to live with Him ; to live with Him means to live to Him. To be reconciled with God by Christ's death means a new creation through His Spirit. Analysis of parts and stages there may be ; distinguishings of inceptions from continuations and continuations from consummations : but to the apostle there is but one salvation, and that salvation is an indivisible whole. The holy life ripening into that perfection without which no

man shall see the Lord, is not with Him an arbitrary
addition to acceptance by God in Christ Jesus, but its
natural and necessary outgrowth : and therefore, with
all his proclamation of life in Christ, the life of faith,
and of an objective salvation in the blood of Jesus, he
never looses sight of the essence of salvation in holiness
of life. So, in our present passage, the whole movement of which turns as on its hinge upon the substitution of Christ for sinners and His death in their
behalf and their consequent righteousness in Him, the
issue of all is found nevertheless in holiness of life.
Those for whom Christ has died are, in their new
creaturehood, to live no longer for themselves but for
Him who died and rose again for them. The revolution
in standing is marked by a revolution in living. If
their trespasses are no longer imputed to them, they
are also no longer to have trespasses to be imputed to
them. In a word, their salvation is not merely from
the penalty but from the power of sin : and the mark
of it is the life that is free not only from the condemnation but from the commission of sin. We are
saved while yet sinners, but not that we may remain
sinners, but that we may glorify God and His saving
power by becoming under His guidance saints.

This is what, according to Paul, we are saved to :
this is what, in his conception of it, salvation is. It is
the promise to us of a perfected life. And surely there

is no promise which could come to us with a more penetrating appeal. There is no one of us so degraded that he would not fain be good : the desire that stirs within us may be so faded and so weak that we can scarcely call it a desire, but we secretly admire the good even when we pursue the bad. Paul points the way not to an inoperative admiration, but to an effective accomplishment. He says to us in effect that all which the best of men have longed for and vainly striven after and the worst have dully admired while impatiently spurning is placed within our reach in Christ Jesus. He says that in Him there is the potency of a new life and that this potency shall surely pass into actualization for all those that are in Him. Or if we choose, we can give form to his message to us to-day rather in the words of his Master and our Master. For what does he say in effect but this : Blessed are they that hunger and thirst after righteousness, for they shall be filled ? For they shall be filled ! Let these words be our encouragement to-day. Let them become from to-day the strength of our life. " They *shall* be *filled !* "

THE GLORIFIED CHRIST

HEBREWS ii. 9 :—But we behold Him who hath been made a little lower than the angels, even Jesus, because of the suffering of death crowned with glory and honour, that by the grace of God He should taste death for every man.

THE GLORIFIED CHRIST

THE words I have chosen as a text form a part of a great passage, the proximate purpose of which is to set in a clear light the surpassing glory of Jesus Christ. In the first chapter of the Epistle to the Hebrews the unapproachable greatness of our Lord's person is exhibited. No mere " interpreter " of God He, like the prophets ; no mere " messenger " of God, like the angels. The Jewish-Christian readers of this Epistle had been prepared by their traditional teaching to expect the coming of a culminating interpreter of God, of a final messenger from God, and they readily greeted Jesus Christ as such. Our author reminds them that, greeting Jesus Christ as such, they had found in Him something much more. No doubt they had found in Him the supreme interpreter of God, who, alone, having seen God, is in a position to " declare " Him,—or, as our author expresses it, who, being the very effulgence of God's glory and the very impress of His substance, can, alone, manifest all that God is. And they had found in Him the final messenger of God who had come to do a service, for the sake of them that shall inherit salvation, which no angel could do, or in His own words, who had come not to be ministered unto but to minister. But our author reminds his readers that they had found in Jesus something more glorious than even these great things, seeing that He had received by inheritance the much more exalted name of Son. The ineffable glory of Jesus Christ lies, he tells us, in this,—that even the great functions of interpreter of God and messenger of God, great as these functions as exercised by Him are, are not the source and not the measure of His greatness. As the Son of God, the effulgence of God's glory, and the impress of God's substance, all the prophets are but His servants, and before His majesty the very angels veil their faces and do Him homage.

The greatness of His work, of course, he now goes on to remind them, corresponds with the greatness of His person. In the second chapter our author advances to exhibit this surpassing greatness of the work of the Son of God. The salvation He wrought is called with pointed directness " so great a salvation," and is contrasted by this epithet with all that even the divinely given law could accomplish. To exhibit its greatness it is set before us in the height of its idea on the positive side. That we are saved by it from sin is taken for granted, and alluded to as a matter well known to all. But the negative side of salvation is not treated as the measure of its greatness. We are asked to attend, not to what we are saved from, but to what we are saved to. And that is presented as nothing less than dominion over the universe. This dominion God has destined for man from the beginning. But man had failed of his destiny. How hopelessly, how dismally, he had failed, none knew better than those the author of this Epistle was addressing,— Jews, who had lost even their Jewish ideals, and were now doubting whether in Christianity they had not lost all. He points them to Jesus as one who had saved them out of this depth to that height. Lordship, —not over " this world," with its troubles and trials, its incompletenesses and make-believes, and after all done, the end of death,—but over the " world to be," was theirs. True, they had not entered as yet into their heritage : the " world to be," by that very token, is not yet. But Jesus had entered upon it ; and in Him they held the reversion to it. " But now, not yet do we see all things subjected to man : but Him who has been made a little lower than angels for the suffering of death, Jesus, we behold crowned with glory and honour, in order that by the grace of God His tasting of death should be for every man." He is on the throne ; and He is there not for Himself but for us. It was for us that He died, nay, that He took upon Himself mortality ; and now He is on the throne that this dreadful experience of death might really avail for us.

Had He only died for us, perhaps salvation might have consisted solely in relief from this penalty of sin which He bore for us. That He ascended out of death to the throne, conquers the throne itself for us. When we behold Jesus on the throne for us, we may see how great a salvation He has wrought for us. For on that throne we too shall sit, not merely in Him but with Him. It has always been the Father's good pleasure to give us the Kingdom ; not apart from the Son but along with that Son who is not ashamed to call us brethren. And because this has always been and still is the Father's will, it behoved Him who orders all things for His own glory, in leading many sons into glory, to bring the leader of their salvation through sufferings to the full accomplishment of His great task.

The verse which we have chosen out of this noble context as our text is so remarkable, even in its form, that we must pause for a moment to observe some of its characteristics. The first thing that strikes us about it is the way in which it takes all the great Christian verities for granted,—not formally asserting them, as if it were instructing us as to their reality, but assuming them as things fully established, which could be counted upon to be fully understood, if only suggested. The Incarnation, the Atoning Death, the Session on the right hand of God, the Kingly rule of the exalted Christ,—all these are in this verse touched upon with clearness, confidence, emphasis. But no one of them is asserted, as if the purpose were to inform us of it. They are all assumed as the common conviction of writer and reader, and built upon as such for the conveyance of the special message of the passage.

Note the simplicity and effectiveness with which this is done. What the text wishes to do is, to put it briefly, to turn our eyes from ourselves to Jesus. But it does not speak of Jesus by His bare name, but designates Him by a descriptive phrase taken from the eighth Psalm which had just been quoted. What is this descriptive phrase? " Him that hath been made a little lower than angels " : " But now, we see not yet all things subjected to him," *i.e.* to man : " but Him who hath been made a little lower than angels, we behold, Jesus." Now, how could this phrase be thus employed to describe Jesus as a man ? You observe, it is not, properly speaking, a " quotation " from the Psalm. It is not employed here in the sense of the Psalm. As it stands in the Psalm, it is a proclamation of man's amazing greatness and dignity : God, it is declared, " made man but little lower than angels, and crowned him with glory and honour." Here, it is not a proclamation of dignity, but a recognition of humiliation : " Him that hath been made a little lower than angels for the suffering of death, we behold, Jesus." It is merely the application of certain words taken out of the Psalm in a new sense to designate Jesus according to a habitual mode of thinking of Him. The writer is making a quick transition, and he feels that when he says, " Him who has been made a little lower than angels," everybody will be struck at once with a little shock of pleased surprise at seeing the words of the Psalm suddenly given a new meaning and will anticipate him in saying to themselves, Why, it is Jesus he means : He was made a little lower than angels when he became man. In other words, the author counts confidently on the doctrine of the Incarnation as present to the thought of his readers, to which he can therefore allude, even in the most unexpected language, with the assurance that they will take his point.

Similarly, he says nothing directly about the Atoning work of Christ, but simply alludes to it in a word or two which in themselves might bear a less profound significance, but which he knows cannot but be taken in just this meaning by his readers : " Him," he says, " who hath been made a little lower than angels, for the suffering of death." He speaks only of death. Other men besides Jesus have suffered death : every other man, sooner or later, suffers death. In themselves the words, therefore, carry no

suggestion of anything unusual in Jesus' case. But
the writer knew that every Christian heart would
respond, when he spoke of Jesus suffering death, and
that with a turn of phrase which called attention to
the suffering which He endured in His death, with a
thrill of joyful recognition that this suffering of death
was not merely the usual payment of the debt of
nature, common to man, but was fraught with high
significance. This indeed, he subtly suggests, by
speaking of Jesus' becoming a little lower than angels
for the suffering of death : it was for this purpose
that He became man,—that He might endure this
death. Other men do not become men to die : Jesus
did—and in this he separated Himself from man.
Death to Him is His voluntary act, and must be
endured, not of necessity, but for an end. With such
a suggestion embedded in it, our author can easily
trust his bare mention of the death of Jesus to suggest
forcibly to his readers all that a full reference to the
atonement could convey.

The same is true of his allusion to the Ascension.
Of the Ascension itself he says nothing, nor of the
Resurrection which preceded it and forms its presupposition. He merely says, still in words borrowed
from the description of man's high destiny in the
eighth Psalm, that Jesus has been " crowned with
glory and honour." With what sort of glory ? With

what kind of honour ? Perhaps the glory and honour of the grateful memory of men ? The inscription of His name on some monument, in some hall of fame ? Or, possibly, on the hearts of His grateful followers ? Does he mean that all history will ring with His praise, and, like the widow who cast in her mite at the treasury of the Temple, this that He did shall be remembered in His honour through all generations ? Nothing of the kind. He means the actual session of Jesus upon the throne of the universe, that He may reign with a real rule over all principalities and powers and mights and dominions. But the words which he employs do not themselves say this. That he leaves to the natural understanding of his readers, whom he knows he can trust to read into his bare allusion to the crowning of Jesus with glory and honour the whole body of facts concerning His exaltation, including His resurrection and ascension and session at the right hand of God, thence expecting till He shall make His enemies His footstool.

You see how remarkable our text is for its confident dealing with this great circle of Christian doctrines by way of allusion. It is as plain as day that these things were not novelties to the writer or to his readers. They were not things about which he felt that he must instruct his readers ; or even which they required to be reminded of in detail. They were things which stood to them and himself, alike, as the basis of their faith and hope. It is, therefore, also clear that these doctrines, thus suggested by way of allusion, do not constitute the specific teaching of our text. We do not deal with our main purpose in writing by way of allusion. The burden of the text is found, therefore, not in these great doctrines of the Incarnation, the Atonement, the Session at the right hand of God, which are brought before us in it, richly, powerfully, movingly, indeed, but, in point of mode of presentation, allusively. It is to be found in the final clause of the text, up to which they lead, and which describes the purpose, for which the incarnated Son of God, having become man and suffered death, has been crowned with glory and honour. This purpose was—I re-translate the words in an effort to bring out their true sense and relations—" in order that this, His bitter experience of death, may by the grace of God redound to the benefit of every man."

As it is in these words that the real message of the text is delivered to us, they demand our most careful scrutiny. To place them in their proper relation, let us observe in the first place that the clause goes back to the preceding words, " Because of the suffering of death " ; and finds its true sense only when read in reference to them. Jesus Christ became man that He might die ; and He has been crowned with glory and honour that this, His death, might by God's grace redound to the benefit of man. We are justified in rendering the strong Greek verb—" that He may taste of death "—by the strong English substantive —" that His bitter experience of death," on the general rule, which used to be so fertilely emphasized by Edward Thring, that it is the verb in the one language and the substantive in the other that is the strong word, and that our translations, if they are to be true to the stress of the original, must bear this in mind.

But perhaps it is worth while to pause to point out that the idea intended to be conveyed by the phrase " tasting of death " is a strong and not a weak one. Many, no doubt, when they read of our Lord's " tasting death," take it as implying that He merely " had a taste of death," as we say,—passed through it with the minimum of conscious experience of its terror. Precisely the contrary is what is really meant. What the phrase signifies is that He was not a merely passive subject of death, of whom it is merely to be said that He died, and that is all of it : but that He drained this bitter cup to its dregs. It is the horror and the pains of death that are thrown up boldly for our con-templation by this phrase ; and therefore it is used to take up again the preceding phrase,—" the suffering of death," a phrase which by an unexpected turn of

expression itself emphasizes the sufferings of death.
Jesus became a man not merely that He might suffer
death, but that He might endure the sufferings of
death. He was not merely the object on which death
wrought ; He in dying suffered, had strong agonies
to endure. And now, our present clause adds that
this dreadful cup of death was drunk by Him, for a
high end,—that by God's grace benefits might be
secured for men.

Let us not pass on too rapidly to remind ourselves that in these words lies the emphasis not
only of our text, but of this entire Epistle. For one
of the great objects of this Epistle was to exhibit the
glory of the death of Christ. To those old Jewish
Christians for whom the Epistle was written, the
offence of Jesus was—what the offence of Jesus has
been ever since to all who, though not of Jewish blood,
are of Jewish hearts—just the cross. Jesus as God's
" interpreter," the supreme prophet, revealing by
word and deed what God is and what God intends for
man : Jesus as God's " messenger," the supernal
agent in the divine work of gathering His people to
Himself : these were ideas familiar to them, to which
they gave immediate and glad hospitality. But Jesus,
the bruised and broken sufferer hanging on the accursed
tree,—it was hard for them to adjust themselves to
that ; and this it was which, first of all things, as the

cruelties of their lot shook their courage and faith,
they were in danger of drifting away from. This it
was, therefore, which, first of all things, the author of
this Epistle desired to fix in their hearts as too precious
to lose hold of ; as, indeed, the very centre and core
of their Christianity, first spoken by the Lord Himself,
and confirmed to them by those who heard Him,
God bearing witness with them with signs and wonders
and divers miracles and gifts of the Holy Ghost, dis-
tributed according to His will. And therefore he gives
his strength in the paragraph of which our text forms
a part to carrying home to them these two great
truths : that it became God—seeing that He it is
to whom all things tend as their end and through
whom all things come to pass as their director and
governor,—without whom, therefore, as end and means,
nothing takes place—to lead many sons to glory ; and
that it became Him equally to make the Leader in
their salvation perfect—that is, to bring His saving
work to the completion which is its accomplishment—
through suffering. These are the two ideas, you will
perceive at once, which, though they are announced
in the form in which I have just stated them only in
the next verse, yet already dominate our text. For
precisely what our text seeks to emphasize is that
Jesus passed through sufferings to glory ; and that
the reason why these sufferings were crowned with

glory was in order that they might be made to inure to the benefit of every one.

There still remain two or three points which require, elucidation before the precise message of the text may be grasped with clearness. Perhaps the first of these that will strike us is that the text does not directly announce the reason why Jesus suffered. As I have already pointed out, it does not say explicitly that Jesus suffered that many might enter into glory; but rather only that He has been crowned with honour and glory that His sufferings might inure to the good of every one. For all that is openly asserted in this verse by itself, it might be plausibly argued that the saving power of Jesus resided in His session at the right hand of God, rather than in His death; though no doubt we should be given pause in pushing this notion by observing that after all His kingly power is not represented as itself the saving force, but only as needed to secure its proper efficacy to His death: " That the bitterness of His death should inure to the good of every one." And the context speedily supplies all that may be thought wanting in the text itself. We are immediately told that it was becoming in our Lord as the Leader in our salvation to partake in all that belongs to those whom He would lead to glory, since only so could he open the way for them to this glory: He must through death bring to naught Him that had the power of death, that is the devil, and deliver all them who through fear of death were all their lifetime subject to bondage. Obviously it is sin that blocks the way to their ascent to glory, and soon we find it expressly declared that the reason why our Lord was made in all things like unto His brethren was that as a merciful and faithful high priest He might make propitiation for the sins of the people. We must not, therefore, infer from the absence of express mention of it in our text that the author of our Epistle did not look upon the sufferings and death of Christ as primarily and above all the expiation of sin : or imagine that this idea does not underlie and colour the language of the text and need not be held in mind by us as part of its presupposition. On the contrary, this is one of the main foundations, as of the whole argument of the Epistle, so of our text as well.

Meanwhile it is not thrown forward in our text, and the reason is, as has already been intimated, that the aspect of salvation which is for the moment engrossing the mind of the author is not that of deliverance from the curse of sin. He is looking at salvation at this point of his argument not on its negative, but on its positive side. His mind is not full at the moment of what man is saved from, but with what man is saved to. He cannot help speaking of the sufferings of Christ, and throwing these sufferings out in the highest relief : for it was in and through these sufferings that Christ saved us. But His eye is set, not on the depths out of which this salvation has raised us, but on the heights to which it promises to elevate us. This is what is swelling in his heart when he calls it " so great salvation." And the specific aspect of its greatness which is occupying his attention is the universal dominion which it brings to saved mankind. O the greatness of this salvation, which Jesus Christ has wrought for us, he seems to cry ; by it we are elevated well-nigh to the throne of God itself, and all creation is placed beneath our feet !

It is especially important to note the completeness of the writer's preoccupation at this point with the positive side of salvation, and, indeed, with the particular aspect of the positive side of salvation which consists in the establishing of mankind in its destined dominion over the creation, in order that we may understand another peculiarity of his exposition. This is the apparent inclusion of Christ Himself among those who share in the salvation adverted to. Nothing could be further from our author's mind than that theory of the atonement, sometimes vividly called the theory of " salvation by sample," which conceives our Lord in His incarnation to have taken sinful flesh, and to have participated in His own work of saving humanity from sin. Our author is express

in his assertion that our Lord was "without sin,"
although He was offered specifically to bear the sins of
many; and He makes it a part of our Lord's superi-
ority to the priest of the shadow-dispensation that He
did not require as the priest did to offer sacrifice for
Himself as well as for the people. Our author no more
than the other writers of the New Testament imagined
Jesus to participate in His own propitiation for sin.
Yet, in this context, he speaks of Him as "the Leader
in salvation," making use of a term variously rendered,
"Author," "Captain," "Prince," of salvation, which
may seem to imply that He leads in salvation because
He is the first to take part in it, as well as the principal
cause of it; as we may speak of a bad man as the
leader in all the evil in which a coterie under his
influence indulges; or, more appropriately in this
connection, of a good man as the leader in all the good
works his example inspires; or, even better still, of a
great popular saviour like Washington as the leader
of his people into freedom and power. And, indeed,
our whole passage is cast in some such mould as this.
For what does it do but bid us see in the exaltation of
Jesus to the throne of the universe, the fulfilment in
principle of the promise in the Psalm of universal
dominion to man, which is here identified with the
great salvation earned by Christ? The explanation
of this apparent inclusion of Jesus Himself in His own

saving work, is found in the engrossment of the writer with the positive aspect of salvation, and that as manifested in dominion over the creation, to the exclusion for the moment of contemplation of its whole negative side.

The negative aspect of salvation, no doubt, enters too deeply into the very essence of salvation ever to be wholly out of mind when the work of Christ is spoken of. And therefore, though the immediate interest of the writer, in our text, rests not so much on the relation of Christ's death to the guilt which it expiates, as on its relation to the glory which it purchases, yet he not only alludes to His death, but throws it into prominence as the basis of all that Jesus has obtained for men. And certainly there is no forgetfulness apparent that it was for others, not for Himself, that all our Lord's work was done. The very purpose for which the whole passage was written is to emphasize the fact that it was not for Himself but for others that our Lord wrought : and that purpose is nowhere more emphatically asserted than in this very culminating clause of our text, the assertion of which is precisely that our Lord's bitter experience of death was on behalf of others : " In order that, thus, His tasting of death might by God's grace inure to the benefit of every man." The energy of this expression is so great, in fact, that we may possibly

be misled by it into attaching a meaning to it which
was certainly not intended by its author. By his use
here of the term " every man "—" in order that He
might taste of death for every man "—the author has
no intention of asserting a universal salvation. As we
are reminded by a recent commentator, he "nowhere
expresses hope or expectation of universal redemption."
His interest is not in asserting that each and every
man who lives in the world, or has lived or will live in
it, shall attain to the universal dominion promised
through the Psalmist. He knows very well that this
will not be the case ; no one could be more earnest
than he is in warning his readers against neglecting
this great salvation and incurring the fate of thorns
and thistles whose end is to be burned. And the
refinement of a universal redemption which does not
take universal effect, but hangs for its realization
upon a condition to be fulfilled by the redeemed themselves, is foreign to his whole thought. He is speaking
in our text moreover not of the intention with which
Christ died, but of the realization of that intention
through the power of the ascended Christ. His interest
is absorbed in the contrast between Jesus' earning the
promised dominion for Himself alone, and His earning
it for others. What he asserts, and that with the
highest energy, is that Jesus did not act for Himself in
the great transaction which he speaks of as this " so

great salvation," but for others : and that the result
of it is not that by it He Himself attained to honour
and glory, but that He by it led a multitude of sons
of God into glory. And therefore the " every one "
of this verse is immediately translated into the " many
sons " of the next : " For it became Him, for whom
are all things, and through whom are all things, to
bring many sons into glory."

Certainly there is a sense in which this " every one "
is the human race. Jesus' endurance of death for
every one is set forth as the ground on which the
fulfilment of the Psalmist's promise is based. And
that promise was that to man should be give dominion
over creation. The nerve of the assertion our author
makes is that Christ's ascension to His glory is in
order that His death, suffered on earth, should bring
about this great consummation : " In order that by
God's grace His endurance of death may be for every
one,"—that is, may redound to the glorification, the
establishment on its destined throne, not of Himself,
but of the human race. The promise is to the human
race ; Christ is but the instrument of securing its
fulfilment to the race. He enters His glory not for
Himself, any more than He died for Himself ; but
that He might bring about the glorification of the
race. " Every one " means here, thus, simply the
race at large, and its peculiar form is not intended to

distribute the race into its units, and to declare that
the consummation shall fail for no one of these units ;
but with the greatest possible energy to assert the racial
effect of our Lord's work. Not for Himself, but for
man it was that He died; not for Himself, but for man
it was that He has ascended into heaven and has
seated Himself on the right hand of God ; not for
Himself, but for man is it that He has been crowned
with glory and honour, that His death may not be of
no effect, but by God's grace His endurance of death
may inure to the benefit of mankind.

And now, perhaps, we are prepared tardily to throw
into its proper relief the especial message of the text
for us. What is it but this : The necessity of the
exaltation of Christ for the completion of His saving
work ? We are accustomed to think of Christ dying
for us. Let us remember that He not only died for us,
but rose again for us : Paul says that He who was
delivered up for our trespasses was raised for our
justification. And let us remember that He was not
only raised for us, but ascended into heaven for us
and sits at the right hand of God for us. It was
therefore that our Lord declared that it was expedient
for us that He should go away, and that Paul exhorts
us to remember Jesus Christ, risen from the dead, of
the seed of David. What our author does when he
declares that we behold Jesus, made a little lower than

angels for the suffering of death, crowned with glory
and honour, that His bitter experience of death may
be for the benefit of every one, is to fix our eyes on the
saving work of the exalted Jesus. If He died to expiate
our sins, He reigns in heaven that He may apply the
benefits accruing from that expiation to His people,
and may thus bring them into the glory He has purchased for them. If, says Paul, while we were enemies,
we were reconciled with God through the death of His
Son, much more, being reconciled, shall we be saved
by His life. Christ no more died for us two thousand
years ago at Calvary, than He now lives for us in
heaven.

An exhortation to fix our eyes on the exalted
Saviour was eminently timely when this Epistle was
written ; and it is no less timely to-day after the
passage of these two thousand years. Then, the
Hebrew Christians, puzzled and distressed by the
spectacle of a suffering Christ, needed to have their
hearts cheered and their faith steadied by the great
vision of the exalted Christ : they needed to be con-
tinually reminded that Jesus died, not for Himself
but for man, and that His death cannot fail of its high
purpose, seeing that He Himself, sitting on the throne
of the universe, will see to it that the seed that was
sown in sorrow shall produce a harvest which shall be
reaped in joy : He shall see of the travail of His soul

and be satisfied. And we to-day, in the special trials to faith which an age of critical doubt has brought to us, need to keep in constant remembrance that our trust is put not in a dead, but in a living Christ,—in a Christ who died, indeed, but whom the tomb could not retain, but lo! He is alive for evermore. The fashionable, I do not say unbelief, I say the fashionable belief, about us to-day, forgets or neglects, or openly turns its back upon the living Christ, and bids us seek inspiration for our lives and hope for our future, in a Jesus who lived and died in Palestine two thousand years ago,—and that was all. Dimly seen through the ever-increasing obscurity of the gathering years, that great figure has still the power to attract the gaze and to quicken the pulses—yes, to dominate the lives—of men. This is, no doubt, much ; but so little is it all, that it is the least of what we are to seek and to find in Jesus Christ. He is our inspiration ; and, knowing Him better than these, our would-be guides, know Him, He is also our example. But He is so much more than our inspiration or even our example, that we need scarcely think of these things when we think of Him : He is our life. And He is our life not only because He has washed out in His blood the death-warrant that had been issued against us—giving, as He Himself phrased it, His life as a ransom for many— but also because, after He had purchased us to Himself by His precious blood, He has become to us the living fountain and ever-flowing source of life and blessedness. Jesus on the cross is our Saviour ; and it is our privilege to behold Him on His cross, an all-sufficient sacrifice for our sins. But Jesus on His throne is our Saviour too ; and it is our privilege to-day, as we read the lofty words of this great declaration of the Epistle to the Hebrews, to behold Him on His throne, crowned with glory and honour, that His tasting of death may by God's grace be the actual salvation of our souls.

Let us fix our eyes and set our hearts to-day, then, on our exalted Saviour. Let us see Him on His throne made head over all things to His Church, with all the reins of government in His hands,—ruling over the world, and all the changes and chances of time, that all things may work together for good to those that love Him. Let us see Him through His spirit ruling over our hearts, governing all our thoughts, guiding all our feelings, directing all our wills, that, being His, saved by His blood, we may under His unceasing control steadily work out our salvation, as He works in us both the willing and the doing, in accordance with His good pleasure. As, in our unrighteousness, we know we have an Advocate with the Father, Jesus Christ the righteous,—or, as our own Epistle puts it, a great High Priest who has entered within the veil and ever liveth to make intercession there for us : so let us know that in our weakness we have the protecting arm of the King of kings and Lord of lords about us, and He will not let us slip, but will lose none that the Father has given Him, but will raise them up at the last day. Having been tempted like as we are (though without sin), He is able to sympathize with us in our infirmities ; having suffered as we do, He knows how to support us in our trials ; and having opened a way in His own blood leading to life, He knows how to conduct our faltering steps that we may walk in it. Christ our Saviour is on the throne. The hands that were pierced with the nails of the cross wield the sceptre. How can our salvation fail ?

> Art thou afraid His power shall fail
>   When comes thine evil day ?
> Or can an all-creating arm
>   Grow weary, or decay ?
>
> Supreme in wisdom as in power,
>   The Rock of Ages stands ;
> Though Him thou canst not see, nor trace
>   The workings of His hands.

What matters it if we cannot see ? There is a firmer foundation for confidence here than sight. " Who shall separate us from the love of Christ ? shall tribulation, or anguish, or persecution, or famine, or nakedness, or peril, or sword ? . . . Nay, in all these things we are more than conquerors through Him that loved us. For I am persuaded that neither death, nor life, nor angels, nor principalities, nor things present, nor things to come, nor powers, nor height, nor depth, nor any other creature, shall be able to separate us from the love of God, which is in Christ Jesus our Lord." Let us bless God to-day that we can behold Jesus, not only made a little lower than the angels for the suffering of death, but, having suffered death for us, crowned with glory and honour, that by God's grace the bitter pains He suffered in our behalf may be efficacious for the saving of our souls.

Just one word, in closing, especially to you who have given yourselves to the service of Christ in the ministry of His grace. Remember that you serve a living, not a dead Christ. You are to trust in His blood. In it alone have you life. But you are to remember that He was not broken by death, but broke death ; and having purchased you to Himself by His blood, now rules over your souls from His heavenly throne. He is your master whom you are to obey. He has given you commandment to bring all peoples to the knowledge of Him. And He has promised to be with you, even to the end of the world. Live with Him. Keep fast hold upon Him ; be in complete touch with Him. Let your hearts dwell with Him in the heavenly places, that the arm of His strength may be with you in your earthly toil. Let this be that by which all men know you : that in good report and in bad, in life and in death, in the great and in the small affairs of life—in everything you do down to the minutest acts of your everyday affairs— you are the servants of the Lord Christ. So will you be truly His disciples, and so will He be your Saviour —unto the uttermost.

THE RISEN JESUS

2 TIMOTHY ii. 8 :—Remember Jesus Christ, risen from the dead.

THE RISEN JESUS

THE opening verses of the second chapter of the
Second Epistle to Timothy are in essence a comprehensive exhortation to faithfulness. The apostle Paul
was lying imprisoned at Rome, with expectation of no
other issue than death. The infant Church had fallen
upon perilous times. False teachers were assailing
the very essence of the Gospel. Defection had invaded
the innermost circle of the apostle's companions.
Treachery had attacked his own person. Over against
all these dreadful manifestations of impending destruction, he strenuously exhorts his own son in faith,
Timothy, to steadfast faithfulness. Faithfulness to
himself, faithfulness to the cause he had at heart,
faithfulness to the truth as he preached it, faithfulness
to Jesus Christ, their common Redeemer and Lord.

The temptations to unfaithfulness by which Timothy
was assailed were very numerous and very specious.
Many good men had fallen and were falling victims to
them. The perverted teachings of the errorists of the
day were urged with a great show of learning and with
eminent plausibility. And they were announced with
a fine scorn which openly declared that only dull wits
could rest in the crude ideas with which Paul had faced
the world—and lost. The sword of persecution had

been ruthlessly unsheathed, and sufferings and a cruel death watched in the way of those who would fain walk in the path Paul had broken out. It seemed as if the whole fabric which the apostle had built up at such cost of labour and pain was about to fall about his ears.

Paul does not for a moment, however, lose courage, either for himself, or for his faithful followers. But neither does he seek to involve Timothy unwittingly in the difficulties and dangers in which he found himself. He rather bids him first of all to count the whole cost. And then he points him to a source of strength which will supply all his needs. We called the passage an exhortation. We might better call it, more specifically, an encouragement. And the encouragement culminates in a very remarkable sentence. This sentence is pregnant enough to reveal at once the central thought of Paul's Gospel and the citadel of his own strength. Amid all the surrounding temptations, all the encompassing dangers, Paul bids Timothy to bear in mind, as the sufficing source of abounding strength, the great central doctrine,—or rather, let us say, the great central fact—of his preaching, of his faith, of his life. And he enunciates this great fact, in these words : Jesus Christ raised from the dead, of the seed of David.

It is, of course, to the glorified Jesus that Paul

directs his own and Timothy's gaze. Or, to be more specific, it is to the regal lordship of the resurrected Jesus that he points as the Christian's strength and support. The language is compressed to the extremity of conciseness. It is difficult to convey its full force except in diluted paraphrase. Paul bids Timothy in the midst of all the besetting perplexities and dangers which encompassed him to strengthen his heart by bearing constantly in remembrance, not Jesus Christ *simpliciter*, but Jesus Christ conceived specifically as the Lord of the Universe, who has been dead, but now lives again and abides for ever in the power of an endless life ; as the royal seed of David ascended in triumph to His eternal throne. It is not from the exaltation of Jesus alone, let us observe, that Paul draws and would have Timothy draw strength to endure in the crisis which had fallen upon their lives. It is to the contrast between the past humiliation and the present glory of the exalted Lord that he directs his eyes. He does not say simply, " Bear in mind that Jesus Christ sits on the throne of the universe and all things are under His feet," although, of course, it is the universal dominion of Jesus which gives its force to the exhortation. He says, " Bear in mind that Jesus Christ has been raised from the dead, of the seed of David—that it is He that died who, raised from the dead, sits as eternal king in the heavens." No doubt a part of the apostle's object in his allusion to the past humiliation of the exalted Lord is to constitute a connection between Jesus Christ and his faithful followers, that they may become imitators of Him. They, the *viatores*, may see in Him, the *consummator*, one who like them had Himself been *viator*, and may be excited to follow after Him that they too may in due time become *consummatores*. But the nerve of the exhortation, obviously, does not lie in this, as the very language in which it is couched sufficiently avouches. How could Timothy imitate our Lord in being of the seed of David ? How could he imitate Him by ascending the throne of the universe ? Fundamentally the apostle is pointing to Christ not as our example, but as our almighty Saviour. He means to adduce the great things about Him. And the central one of the great things he adduces about Him is that He has been raised from the dead.

It is not to be overlooked, of course, that Paul adverts to the resurrection of Christ here with his mind absorbed not so much in the act of His rising as in its issues. " Bear in mind," he says, " Jesus Christ, as one who has been raised from the dead " : that is to say, as one who could not be holden of the grave, but has burst the bonds of death, and lo ! He lives for evermore. But neither can it be overlooked that it is specifically to the resurrection, which is an act, that he adverts ; and that he adverts to it in such a manner as to make it manifest that the fact of the resurrection of Christ held a place in his Gospel which deserves to be called nothing less than central. The exalted Christ is conceived by him distinctly as the resurrected Jesus ; and it is clear that, had there been no resurrection of Jesus, Paul would not have known how to point Timothy to the exalted Christ as the source of his strength to face with courage the hardships and defeats of life. From this great fact, he derives, therefore, the very phraseology with which he exhorts Timothy, with rich reference to all that is involved in Christ our Forerunner, to die with his Lord that he might also live with Him, to endure with Him that he might also reign with Him. To Paul, it is clear, the resurrection of Christ was the hinge on which turned all his hopes and all his confidence, in life and also in death.

Now, there is a sense in which it is of no special importance to lay stress on the place which the resurrection of Christ held in Paul's thought and preaching. In this sense, to wit : that nobody doubts that it was central to Paul's Gospel. It would seem impossible, in fact, to read the New Testament and miss observing that not only to Paul, but to the whole body of the founders of Christianity, the conviction of the reality of Christ's bodily resurrection entered into the very basis of their faith. The fact is broadly spread upon the surface of the New Testament record. Our Lord Himself deliberately staked His whole claim to the credit of men upon His resurrection. When asked for a sign He pointed to this sign as His single and sufficient credential. The earliest preachers of the Gospel conceived witnessing to the resurrection of their Master to be their primary function. The lively hope and steadfast faith which sprang up in them they ascribed to its power. Paul's whole gospel was the gospel of the Risen Saviour : to His call he ascribed his apostleship ; and to His working, all the manifestation of the Christian faith and life.

There are in particular two passages in Paul's Epistles, which reveal, in an almost startling way, the supreme place which was ascribed to the resurrection of Christ by the first believers in the Gospel.

In a context of very special vigour he declares roundly that " if Christ hath not been raised " the apostolic preaching and the Christian faith are alike vanity, and those who have believed in Christ lie yet unrelieved of their sins. His meaning is that the resurrection of Christ occupied the centre of the Gospel which was preached alike by him and all the apostles, and which had been received by all Christians. If, then, this resurrection should prove to be not a real occurrence, the preachers of the Gospel are convicted of being false witnesses of God, the faith founded on their preaching is proved an empty thing, and the hopes conceived on its basis are rendered void. Here Paul implicates with him the whole Christian community, teachers and taught alike, as suspending the truth of Christianity on the reality of the resurrection of Christ. And so confident is he of universal agreement in the indispensableness of this fact to the integrity of the Christian message, that he uses it for his sole fulcrum for prying back the doctrine of the resurrection of believers into its proper place in the faith of his sceptical readers. " If dead men are not raised, neither hath Christ been raised," is his sole argument. And he plies this argument with the air of a man who knows full well that no one who calls himself a Christian will tolerate that conclusion. The fact that Christ has been raised lay firmly embedded in the depths of the Christian consciousness.

In some respects even more striking are the implications of such phraseology as meets us in another passage. Here the apostle is contrasting all the " gains " of the flesh with the one great " gain " of the spirit—Christ Jesus the Lord. As over against " the excellency of the knowledge of Christ Jesus, his Lord," he declares that he esteems " all things " as but refuse,—the heap of leavings from the feast which is swept from the table for the dogs,—if only he may

" gain Christ and be found in Him," if only, he repeats, he may " know Him, and the power of His resurrection, and the fellowship of His sufferings, becoming conformed into His death ; if by any means he may attain to the resurrection from the dead." The structure of the sentence requires us to recognize the very essence of the saving efficacy of Christ as resident in " the power of His resurrection." It is through the power exerted by His resurrection that His saving work takes effect on men. That is to say, Paul discovers the centre of gravity of the Christian hope no less than of the Christian faith in the fact of the resurrection of Christ. And of the Christian life as well. From the great fact that Christ has risen from the dead, proceed all the influences by which Christians are made in life and attainments, here and hereafter, like Him.

In the face of such evidence, spread broadcast over the New Testament, no one has been able to question that the founders of Christianity entrenched themselves in the fact of Christ's resurrection as the central stronghold of their hope, faith, and proclamation. We do not need to lay stress, therefore, on this implication in such a passage as that before us, as if we were seeking proof for a doubtful or even for a doubted fact. The importance of our laying stress on its implication here and its open assertion throughout the New Testament, is that we may be able to estimate the real significance of a very wide-spread tendency which has arisen in our own time to question the importance of this event on which the founders of Christianity laid such great emphasis, and to which they attached such palmary consequence. If nobody doubts that the first preachers of the Gospel esteemed the resurrection of Christ the foundation-stone of their proclamation, the chief stay of their faith and hope alike, there are nevertheless many who do not hesitate to declare roundly that the first preachers of the Gospel were grossly deceived in so esteeming it. This is an inevitable sequence, indeed, of the chariness with respect to the supernatural which so strongly characterizes our modern world. The " unmiraculous Christianity " which has, in one or another of its modes of conception, grown so fashionable in our day, as it could scarcely allow that the most stupendous of all miracles really lay at the basis of Christianity in its historical origins, so cannot possibly allow that confidence in the reality of this stupendous miracle lies to-day at the foundation of the Christian's life and hope. To allow these things would be to confess that Christianity is through and through a supernatural religion—supernatural in its origin, supernatural in its sanctions, supernatural in its operations in the world. And then,—what would become of " unmiraculous Christianity " ?

Accordingly, we have now for more than a whole generation, been told over and over again, and with ever-increasing stridency of voice, that it makes no manner of difference whether Jesus rose from the dead or not. The main fact, we are told, is not whether the body that was laid in the tomb was resuscitated. Of what religious value, we are asked, can that purely physical fact be to any man ? The main fact is that Jesus—that Jesus who lived in the world a life of such transcendent attractiveness, going about doing good, and by His unshaken and unshakable faith in providence revealed to men the love of a Father-God,— this Jesus, though He underwent the inevitable experience of change which men call death, yet still lives. Lives !—lives in His Church ; or at least lives in that heaven to which He pointed us as the home of our Father, and to which we may all follow Him from the evils of this life ; or in any event lives in the influence which His beautiful and inspiring life still exerts upon His followers and through them in the world. This, this, we are told, is the fact of real religious value ; the only fact upon which the religious emotions can take hold ; by which the religious life can be quickened ; and through which we may be impelled to religious effort and strengthened in religious endurance.

The beauty of the language in which these assertions are clothed and the fervour of religious feeling with which it is suffused, must not be permitted to blind us to the real issue that is raised by them. This is not whether our faith is grounded in a mere resuscitation of a dead man two thousand years ago ; or rather in a living Lord reigning in the heavens. It is not the peculiarity of this new view that it focuses men's eyes on the glorified Jesus and bids them look to Him for their inspiration and strength. That is what the apostles did, and what all, since the apostles, who have followed in their footsteps, have done. Paul did not say to Timothy merely, " Remember that Jesus Christ, when He died, rose again from the dead,"—although to have said that would have been to have said much. Directing Timothy's eyes to the glorified Jesus, reigning in power in the heavens, he said, " Remember Jesus Christ, risen from the dead, of the seed of David." It is not, then, the peculiarity of this new view that it has discovered the living and reigning Christ. The living and reigning Christ has always been the object of the adoring faith of Christians. It is its peculiarity that it neglects or denies the resurrected Christ.

It does not pretend that in neglecting or denying the resurrected Christ it does not break with the entirety of historical Christianity. It freely allows that the apostles firmly believed in a resurrected Christ, and that, following the apostles, Christians up

to to-day have firmly believed in a resurrected Christ.
And it freely allows that this firm belief in a resurrected Christ has been the source of much of the
enthusiasm of Christian faith and of the Christian
propaganda through all the ages. But it hardily
affirms that this emphasis on the resurrected Christ
nevertheless involves a gross confusion—no less a
confusion than that of the kernel with the husk.
And it stoutly maintains that the time has come to
shell off the husk and keep the kernel only. Religious
belief, we are told, cannot possibly rest on or be
inseparably connected with a mere occurrence in time
and space. What others have seen in a different age
from ours—what is that to us ? That Jesus rose from
the dead two thousand years ago and was seen of men
—how can that concern us to-day ? All that can
possibly be of any significance to us is that He was
" not swallowed up in death, but passed through
suffering and death to glory, that is, to life, power, and
honour." " Faith has nothing to do with the knowledge of the form in which Jesus lives, but only with
the conviction that He is the living Lord."

Here now is a brand-new conception of the matter,
standing in express contrast, and in expressly acknow-
ledged contrast, with the conception of the founders,
and hitherto of the whole body of the adherents, of
Christianity. It is the outgrowth, as we have already

hinted, of a distaste for the supernatural. To get rid of the supernatural in the origins of Christianity, its entire historical character is surrendered. The Christianity now to be proclaimed is to be confessedly a " new Christianity "—a different Christianity from any which has ever heretofore existed on the face of the earth. And its novelty consists in this, that it is to have no roots in historical occurrences of any kind whatsoever. Religious belief, we are told, must be independent of all mere facts.

We must not forget that the professed purpose of this new determination of the relation of Christianity to fact is to save Christianity. If Christianity is independent of all historical facts, why, it is clear that it cannot be assailed through the medium of historical criticism. Let criticism reconstruct the historical circumstances which have been connected with its origin as it may ; it cannot touch this Christianity which stands out of relation with all historical occurrences whatever. Doubtless it would be a great relief to many minds to be emancipated from all fear of historical criticism. But it is certainly a great price we are asked to pay for this emancipation. The price indeed is no less an one than Christianity itself. For the obvious effect of the detachment of Christianity from all historical fact is to dismiss Christianity out of the realm of fact.

Christianity is a " historical religion," and a " Christianity " wholly unrelated to historical occurrences is just no Christianity at all. Religion,—yes, man may have religion without historical facts to build upon, for man is a religious animal and can no more escape from religion than he can escape from any other of his persistent instincts. He may still by the grace of God know something of God and the soul, moral responsibility and immortality. But do not even the heathen know the same ? And what have we more than they ? We may still call by the name of " Christianity " the tattered rags of natural religion which may be left us when we have cast away all the facts which constitute Christianity,—the age-long preparation for the coming of the Kingdom of God ; the Incarnation of the Son of God ; His atoning death on the Cross ; His rising again on the third day and His ascension to heaven ; the descent of the Spirit on the Pentecostal birthday of the Church. But to do so is to outrage all the proprieties of honest nomenclature. For " Christianity " is not a mere synonym of " religion," but is a specific form of religion determined in its peculiarity by the great series of historical occurrences which constitute the redemptive work of God in this sinful world, among which occurrences the resurrection of Christ holds a substantial and in some respects the key position.

The impossibility of sustaining anything which can be called " Christianity " without embracing in it historical facts, may be illustrated by the difficulty in carrying out their programme which is experienced by men who talk of freeing Christianity from its dependence on facts. For do they not bid us to abstract our minds, indeed, from that imagined resuscitation that occurred in Palestine (if it occurred at all) two thousand years ago, but to focus them nevertheless on the living Jesus, who has survived death and still lives in heaven ? Do they forget that when they say " Jesus " they already say " history " ? Who is this " Jesus " who still lives in heaven, and the fact of whose still living in heaven, having passed through death, is to be our inspiration ? Did He once live on earth ? And, living on earth, did He not manifest that unwavering faith in providence which reveals the Father-God to us ? Otherwise what is it to us that He " still " lives in heaven ? To be free from the entanglements of history ; to be immune from the assaults of historical criticism ; it is not enough to cease to care for such facts as His resurrection : we must cease to care for the whole fact of Jesus. Jesus is a historical figure. What He was, no less than what He did, is a matter of historical testimony. When we turn our backs on historical facts as of no significance to our " Christianity," we must turn our backs as well on Jesus—any Jesus we choose to rescue for ourselves from the hands of historical criticism. He who would have a really " unhistorical Christianity " must know no Jesus whether on earth or in heaven. And surely a Christianity without Jesus is just no Christianity at all.

Christianity then stands or falls with the historical facts which, we do not say merely accompanied its advent into the world, but have given it its specific form as a religion. These historical facts constitute its substance, and to be indifferent to them is to be indifferent to the substance of Christianity. In these circumstances it is a dangerous proceeding to declare this or that one of them of no significance to the Christian religion. Especially is it a dangerous proceeding to single out for this declaration, one in which the founders of Christianity discovered so much significance as they discovered in the resurrection of Christ. When Paul says to us, not " Remember Jesus Christ enthroned in heaven," but " Remember Jesus Christ, risen from the dead, of the seed of David," we surely must pause before we allow ourselves to say, " It is of no importance whether He rose from the dead or not." And if we pause and think but a moment, we certainly shall not fail to set our seal to Paul's judgment of the significance of His rising from the dead to the Christian religion. For once let us cast our minds over the real place which the resurrection of Christ holds in the Christian system and we shall not easily escape the conviction that this fact is fundamental to its entire message.

Let us recall in rapid survey some of the various ways in which the resurrection of Jesus evinces itself as lying at the basis of all our hope and of all the hope of the world.

It is natural to think, first of all, of the place of this great fact in Christian apologetics. Opinions may conceivably differ whether it would have been possible to believe in Christianity as a supernaturally given religion if Christ had remained holden of the grave. But it is scarcely disputable that the fact that He did rise again, being once established, supplies an irrefragable demonstration of the supernatural origin of Christianity, of the validity of Christ's claim to be the Son of God, and of the trustworthiness of His teaching as a Messenger from God to man. In the light of this stupendous miracle, all hesitation with respect to the supernatural accompaniments of the life that preceded it, or of the succeeding establishment of the religion to which its seal had been set,— nay, of the whole preparation for the coming of the Messenger of God who was to live and die and rise again, and of the whole issue of His life and death and resurrection—becomes at once unreasonable and absurd. The religion of Christ is stamped at once from heaven as divine, and all marks of divinity in its preparation, accompaniments, and sequences become at once congruous and natural. From the empty grave of Jesus the enemies of the cross turn away in unconcealable dismay. Christ has risen from the dead! After two thousand years of the most determined assault upon the evidence which establishes it, that fact stands. And so long as it stands, Christianity too must stand as the one supernatural religion. The resurrection of Christ is the fundamental apologetical fact of Christianity.

But it holds no more fundamental place in Christian apologetics than in the revelation of life and immortality which Christianity brings to a dying world. By it the veil was lifted and men were permitted to see the reality of that other world to which we are all journeying. The whole relation they bore to life and death, and the life beyond death, was revolutionized to those who saw Him and companied with Him after He had risen from the dead. Death had no longer any terrors for them : they no longer needed to believe, they knew, that there was life on the other side of death, that the grave was but a sojourning place, and, though their earthly tent-dwelling were dissolved, they had a building of God, a house not made with hands, eternal in the heavens.

And we who have come later may see with their eyes and handle with their hands the Word of Life. We can no longer speak of a bourne from which no traveller e'er returns. The resurrection of Christ has broken the middle wall of partition down and only a veil now separates earth from heaven. That He who has died has been raised again and ever lives in the completeness of His humanity is the fundamental fact in the revelation of the Christian doctrine of immortality.

Equally fundamental is the place which Christ's resurrection occupies relatively to our confidence in His claims, His teachings, and His promises. The Lord of Life could not succumb to death. Had he not risen, could we have believed Him when He " made Himself equal with God " ? By His resurrection He set a seal on all the instructions which He gave and on all the hopes which He awakened. Had the one sign which He chose failed, would not His declarations have all failed with it ? Is it nothing to us that He who said, " Come unto Me and I will give you rest " ; who has promised to be with those who trust Him " always even unto the end of the world " ; who has announced to us the forgiveness of sins ; has proved that He has power to lay down His life and to take it again ? Whether is it easier to say, " Thy sins be forgiven thee," or " I will arise and walk " ?

That He could not be holden of death, but arose in the power of a deathless life, gives us to know that the Son of Man has power to forgive sins.

And there is a yet deeper truth : the resurrection of Christ is fundamental to the Christian's assurance that Christ's work is complete and His redemption is accomplished. It is not enough that we should be able to say, " He was delivered up for our trespasses." We must be able to add, " He was raised for our justification." Else what would enable us to say, He was able to pay the penalty He had undertaken ? That He died manifests His love and His willingness to save. It is His rising again that manifests His power and His ability to save. We cannot be saved by a dead Christ, who undertook but could not perform, and who still lies under the Syrian sky, another martyr of impotent love. To save, He must pass not merely to but through death. If the penalty was fully paid, it cannot have broken Him, it must needs have been broken upon Him. The resurrection of Christ is thus the indispensable evidence of His completed work, of His accomplished redemption. It is only because He rose from the dead that we know that the ransom He offered was sufficient, the sacrifice was accepted, and that we are His purchased possession. In one word, the resurrection of Christ is fundamental to the Christian hope and the Christian confidence.

It is fundamental, therefore, to our expectation of ourselves rising from the dead. Because Christ has risen, we no more judge that " if one died for all, then all died," " that the body of sin might be done away," than that having died with Him " we shall also live with Him." His resurrection drags ours in its train. In His rising He conquered death and presented to God in His own person the first-fruits of the victory over the grave. In His rising we have the earnest and pledge of our rising : " For if we believe that Jesus died and rose again, even so them also that are fallen asleep in Jesus will He bring with Him." Had Christ not risen could we nourish so great a hope ? Could we believe that what is sown in corruption shall be raised in incorruption ; what is sown in dishonour shall be raised in glory ; what is sown in weakness shall be raised in power ; what is sown a body under the dominion of a sinful self shall be raised a body wholly determined by the spirit of God ?

Last of all, to revert to the suggestion of the words of Paul with which we began, in the resurrection of Christ we have the assurance that He is the Lord of heaven and earth whose right it is to rule and in whose hands are gathered the reins of the universe. Without it we could believe in His love : He died for us. We could believe in His continued life beyond the tomb : who does not live after death ? It might even be possible that we should believe in His victory over evil : for it might be conceived that one should be holy, and yet involved in the working of a universal law. But had he not risen, could we believe Him enthroned in heaven, Lord of all ? Himself subject to death ; Himself the helpless prisoner of the grave ; does He differ in kind from that endless procession of the slaves of death journeying like Him through the world to the one inevitable end ? If it is fundamental to Christianity that Jesus should be Lord of *all ;* that God should have highly exalted Him and given Him the name which is above *every* name ; that in the name of Jesus *every* knee should bow, and *every* tongue confess Him Lord : then it is fundamental to Christianity that death too should be subject to Him and it should not be possible for Him to see corruption. This last enemy too He must needs, as Paul asserts, put under His feet ; and it is because He has put this last enemy under His feet that we can say with such energy of conviction that nothing can separate us from the love of God which is in Christ Jesus our Lord, —not even death itself : and that nothing can harm us and nothing take away our peace.

O the comfort, O the joy, O the courage, that dwells in the great fact that Jesus is the Risen One, of the seed of David ; that as the Risen One He has become Head over all things ; and that He must reign until

He shall have put all things under His feet. Our brother, who has like us been acquainted with death, —He it is who rules over the ages, the ages that are past, and the ages that are passing, and the ages that are yet to come. If our hearts should fail us as we stand over against the hosts of wickedness which surround us, let us encourage ourselves and one another with the great reminder : Remember Jesus Christ, risen from the dead, of the seed of David !

THE GOSPEL OF THE COVENANT

JOHN vi. 38–39 :—For I am come down from heaven, not to do Mine own will, but the will of Him that sent Me. And this is the will of Him that sent Me, that of all that which He hath given Me I should lose nothing, but should raise it up at the last day.

THE GOSPEL OF THE COVENANT

In the miracle of the feeding of the five thousand our Lord presented Himself symbolically to man as the food of the soul. For, as Augustine reminds us, though the miracles wrought by our Lord are divine works, intended primarily to raise the mind from visible things to their invisible author, yet their message is not exhausted by this. They are to be interrogated also as to what they tell us about Christ, and they will be found to have a tongue of their own if we have skill to understand it. " For," he adds, " since Christ is Himself the Word of God, even a deed of the Word is a word to us." One of His miracles is accordingly not to be treated as a mere picture, which we may be satisfied to look upon and praise ; but rather as a writing, which we are not content to praise though we delight in its beauty, but find no satisfaction until we have read and understood it. We may possibly consider Augustine's detailed decipherment of the signs in which this miracle is written somewhat fanciful. He discovers in it a complete parable of the salvation of man and of men. But we can scarcely refuse, as we read it in the pregnant record of John, to say in Pauline phrase, " These things contain an allegory."

As such, indeed, John presents it. This is the meaning of his care to tell us, as he introduces his recital, that " the passover was at hand " ; not a mere chronological note, we may be sure ; nor yet merely an explanation of the presence of the multitude, gathered for the pilgrimage to Jerusalem ; but a premonition of what is to come,—John's account of the occasion and meaning of the miracle, which itself was the occasion of the great discourse on the bread of life. Christ, the true passover, chose the passover time, when men's minds were upon the type, to present the antitype to them in symbol and open speech. It was therefore also that He tested His disciples with searching questions, designed to bring them to the discovery of whether they yet knew Him ; and that He taxed the people that " signs " were wasted upon them, and that while they were demanding a sign that they might see and believe, the sign had been given them, and though they had seen, they did not believe. It was therefore above all, that Christ followed up the miracle with the wonderful discourse in which He explains the sign, and declares Himself openly to be " the bread of God that cometh down from heaven and giveth life to the world." This is the tremendous truth which miracle and discourse united to proclaim to the multitudes gathered on the shores of Gennesaret at that passover season ; but which, despite type and sign and teaching—each a manifest word from God,—

they could neither receive nor understand. And this is the blessed truth which our text,—taken from the centre of the discourse and constituting, indeed, its kernel,—presents to our apprehension and belief anew to-day. May the Spirit of truth, who searches all things, even the deep things of God, illuminate our minds and prepare our hearts, that we may understand and believe.

Let us begin by observing the testimony borne by our Lord and Master here to His heavenly origin and descent : " I am come down from heaven," He says. And the truth here declared is the foundation of the entire discourse. The whole gist of it is to represent Jesus as the " bread out of heaven," " the true bread out of heaven," " the bread of God that cometh down out of heaven," which the Father hath given for the life of the world. I need not remind you how this representation pervades John's Gospel,—from the testimony of the Baptist, that He who was to supplant him " cometh from above," and is therefore " above all," to Jesus' own triumphant declaration at the close of His life, that, His work being finished, He is ready to return to the Father who sent Him, and to the glory that He had with Him before the world was. Our present asseveration is but a single instance of the constant self-testimony of the Son of Man to His heavenly origin and descent.

The older Unitarianism was prodigal of miracle. It was not the supernatural, but the mysteries of the Holy Trinity and the God-man that were its scandal. When brought face to face with such passages as these, it was wont, therefore, to explain that Jesus, born miraculously of His virgin mother, but a mere man, was taken up to heaven by the divine power to learn the things of God; whence He again descended to bring divine teaching to men. To the newer Unitarianism, on the other hand, it is precisely the supernatural which is the offence. Its philosophical forms might hospitably receive such mysteries as the Trinity and the God-man, if only they may be permitted to run freely into their moulds. But divine interventions of any kind, and most of all the descent of a personal God from heaven to earth, to be incased in flesh and to herd for a season among men, it cannot allow. It therefore attacks our passages with a theory of ideal, not real, pre-existence, and teaches that Jesus means only that, in the thought and intention of God, His advent into the world had long been provided for, and that, in that sense, He was with God and came forth from God.

How weak, how inconceivably banal, all such expedients are before the majesty of Christ's self-witness: " I am come down from heaven." And when we turn over the pages of this Gospel,—the

leading idea of which, it has been said, inadequately
indeed, but so far truly, is the divine glory of Christ
in the incarnation,—and observe our Lord's constant
witness in the discourses recorded in it, not merely to
His descent from the Father, but to His essential
equality and oneness with God, to His eternal pre-
existence with Him, and to His prospective return to
His primal glory with the Father, after His task on
earth is accomplished,—how our spirits bow in worship
before that God only-begotten who is in the bosom
of the Father, who became flesh and tabernacled
among us for a season full of grace and truth, and
by His very existence among us " declared " to us
that God, not only whom He came forth from, but
who He is.

We should not fail to observe, however, that the
incarnation is not spoken of in our text as an end in
itself, but rather as a means to an end. The object of
our Lord here is not to present the bare fact of His
having come down from heaven to the wonder of men,
but to expound the purpose of His coming down from
heaven. " I am come down from heaven," He declares,
" *in order that I may do* the will of Him that sent Me."
You will scarcely need to be reminded that this, too, is
the representation, not of our text only, but of the
whole body of relevant deliverances recorded by John
from the mouth of the Master, and indeed of the entire

Gospel itself. Everywhere and always, it is not the coming down from heaven itself, but the purpose of the coming, that receives the emphasis. And this is why it is inadequate to say that the leading idea of John's Gospel is the glory of Christ in the incarnation. Its leading idea is, rather, the sufficient end of the incarnation, or, in other words, its leading purpose is to present what we may call a satisfactory philosophy of the incarnation.

And this is the precise amount of truth that lies behind the assertion so freely made by those who are stumbled by the heights of John's theology, that his Gospel is not a simple narrative of fact, but an ideological treatise,—which, in their view, is equivalent to saying that it does not give us fact but fancy, and is to be looked upon not as a sober history but as a metaphysical essay. But does history cease to be history when it passes beyond the mere tabulation of events, and essays to marshal them according to their relations and under the categories of cause and effect ?—when it ceases to be a mere chronicle, in a word, and becomes what we have learned to call philosophical history ? And is it to be made a reproach to a writer of history that he has sought not merely to collect, but also to understand his facts ; and to record them in such a way as to bring out their internal nature as well as their external form ?

Bishop Alexander, in his delightful little book on *The Leading Ideas of the Gospels*, places the matter relatively to John's Gospel in a very clear light. " A great life," he reminds us, " cannot be rendered by a simple agglomeration of facts." " A great life,—a life whose words and works influence mankind profoundly, —is not sufficiently told by merely relating its facts and dates. What an enigma, for instance, is the life of Napoleon ! How many of his biographies are mere masks, concealing those bronze features ! We cannot understand any great and complicated life, good or evil, by merely recording the isolated events along which it moved. It is an organic whole, and must be reconstructed as such. . . . This, then, is the great Leading Idea of St. John's Gospel. *Given* the facts of Christ's life, how shall we bind them into unity, and read them as a whole ? What theory of His Person and Nature will give us a logical and consistent view ? . . . What Christ *did* and *said* becomes explicable only by knowing what Christ *is*. . . . Some who have not lost all reverence for Christianity speak as if St. John's prologue added a difficulty for faith ; as if St. Matthew or St. Luke on the incarnation were comparatively easy to receive. Is it so for those who think ? Place side by side these statements. On the one side—' When as His Mother Mary was espoused to Joseph, before they came together she was found with child of the Holy

Ghost.' On the other side, the four oracular proposi-
tions—' In the beginning was the Word, and the Word
was with God, and the Word was God. And the
Word was made flesh.' Which is easier to receive ?
. . . In St. John the fact of the Incarnation is lifted
up and flooded with the light of a divine idea. If in
the Unity of the divine Existence there be a Trinity
of Persons ; if the Second Person of that Trinity is to
assume the reality of flesh and the likeness of sinful
flesh, we can in some measure see why He needed the
tabernacle of a body, framed and moulded by the
Eternal Spirit, to be His fitting habitation. The
mystery of a Virgin Mother is the correlative of the
mystery of the Word made flesh.''

Surely this is most admirably said. To be made
quite perfect, it needs only the removal of the emphasis
from the nature of Christ to the work of Christ. " If
the Second Person of that Trinity is to assume the
reality of flesh, and the likeness of sinful flesh." . . .
Aye, *if*. . . . Dr. Alexander leaves this " *if* " hanging
in the air. But not so John. To give an adequate
account of it is just the object and chief end of his
Gospel. We need to amend the postulation of the
problem, therefore, so far as not only to insert, but to
emphasize this element. " *Given* the facts of Christ's
life, how shall we bind them together into unity, and
read them as a whole ? What theory of His Person

and Nature, and *Purpose* and *Work*, will give us a logical and consistent view ? " This is the problem that John's Gospel answers. And in answering it, it gives us a philosophy of the incarnation, and thus renders not only the incarnation itself, but all that Incarnated Life, not only credible but natural, and not only natural—may we not even say ?—but almost inevitable—impossible to be otherwise. And thus John fulfils the end of his writing : " These are written, that ye may believe that Jesus is the Christ, the Son of God ; and that believing ye may have life in His name."

What, then, is the account of the incarnation which this Gospel thus commends to us as its philosophy ? We note at once that in our text our Lord states it, in the first instance, relatively not to man, but to God. The reason of the incarnation, rendering it credible, natural, inevitable, is traced back into the councils of the Godhead. " I am come down from heaven, not to do My own will, but the will of Him that sent me."

The purpose of the incarnation is therefore primarily to please God the Father, and to perform His will. We cannot avoid the implication that the incarnated one comes, therefore, in a *subordinate* capacity. He came down from heaven not to do His own will, but the will of Him that sent Him. He was sent. He was given a commission, a work, to do. How this conception is repeated over and over again in the discourses recorded by John! Even to John the Baptist He is the "sent of God." When Nicodemus approached Him as a teacher come from God, He explained that He was not come primarily as a teacher, but as one sent by God to do a work. And this is the burden of the great discourses at the pool of Bethesda, at the feast of Tabernacles, on the Light of the World, and as well of the closing discourses at the last passover. In all alike Jesus is the sent of God, come not of Himself to seek His own will, but to do the will of Him that sent Him; and only when He had "accomplished the work given Him to do" to return to the Father who sent Him.

Now this subordinate relation in which Jesus thus pervasively represents Himself as standing to the Father, so as to have been sent by Him, must be a matter either of nature or of arrangement. It must be either essential or economic. It must find its account and origin either in the necessity of nature or else in the provisions of a plan. But side by side with this perfectly pervasive proclamation of His subordination to the Father, in the whole matter of the incarnation itself, and the purpose or "will" that lies behind that incarnation and gives it its justification and its philosophical account, there runs an equally pervasive assertion by Jesus Himself and by His historian as well, of His essential equality and oneness with God. He was not only in the beginning with God : He was God. He is the only-begotten God, who is in the bosom of the Father. To have seen Him is to have seen the Father also. He draws and receives from Thomas the worshipping cry, " My Lord and my God." He declares to the Jews, " I and the Father are One." It seems to be clear, therefore, that the subordination in which the Father is recognized as greater than He, prescribing a " will " for Him to come into the world to perform, is economic, not essential ; a matter of arrangement, not of necessity of nature.

By such a representation we are, of course, carried at once back into the darkness, or, what is equally blinding, into the blaze of mystery. It may be thought that it is enough to be asked to believe in the mysteries of the God-man and of the Trinity,—that within the unity of the Godhead there exists such a distinction of persons that of each we may assert in turn that from the beginning he has been with God, and has been God. Are we to add this additional mystery of fancying the persons of the Godhead, though numerically one in essence and sharers in all the divine attributes, " act-ing," as Dr. Martineau puts it, " each on the other as outside beings and conducting a divine drama among

themselves,"—imposing tasks on one another, re-
quiring conditions of one another, and earning favours
from one another ? No doubt it is past our compre-
hension. But do we gain or lose by denying its possibility, its reality ? What does the Trinity mean, if it
does not mean such a distinction of persons that each
may say relatively to the other, " I," and " Thou,"
and " He " ? What can the incarnation of the Second
Person mean, if the persons may not stand over
against one another in a measure far transcending our
power to comprehend ? And let us remember that
John presents this conception to us, not as an added
difficulty to faith, but as the philosophy, the explanation of the incarnation. It may well happen here, too,
that two mysteries support and render credible each
the other,—as two beams of wood, neither of which
could stand easily alone, when bowed together not
only support each other, but provide a firm foundation upon which you may safely pile the weight of a
slated roof. To adopt Bishop Alexander's mode of
statement,—" If in the Unity of the Divine Existence
there be a Trinity of Persons, and if the Second Person
of that Trinity is to assume the reality of flesh and the
likeness of sinful flesh,"—is it an additional difficulty
or an aid to faith in this supernal mystery to be further
told that this colossal humiliation of the Son of God
was not an objectless display of arbitrary power, nor

yet a tentative and unconsidered effort of divine compassion to do somewhat, as yet undetermined in kind or amount, for sinful mankind, but the execution in time of an eternal plan,—a plan born of, and redolent in its every part with the infinite compassion of God, shaped in all its details from all eternity by brooding love, and now remaining only to be executed by each person involved taking and completing his appointed part in its tremendous work? The mystery of the covenant is the correlative of the mystery of the incarnation. Without its postulation the incarnation would present increased difficulties of belief. Without the added words, " In order to do the will of Him that sent Me," the declaration, " I am come down from heaven," would remain a simple marvel and prove a strain on faith.

And now let us not fail to observe that it results from what we have said, that John's Gospel is the Gospel of the Covenant. If its leading idea is not merely the glory of the incarnation, but the philosophy of the incarnation ; and if that philosophy runs back into an economic arrangement or plan between the Persons of the Trinity, by which the Second Person comes to perform a work committed to Him by the Father, not to do His own will, but the will of Him that sent Him : this is but another way of saying that the leading idea of John's Gospel is the idea of the Covenant. And is it not so ?   Search and look, and you will find not only that this covenant idea recurs again and again throughout the Gospel, with a frequency and an emphasis which throw it well into the foreground, but that the book, as a whole, is moulded in its form and contents upon it. The burden of its first chapters is Christ's testimony that He has come because sent by the Father ; the burden of the last chapters is His approaching return to the Father who sent Him ; the accomplished work lies between. And therefore it is that when Nicodemus came to Him at the opening of His ministry and asked for teaching, Jesus pointed him rather to His work, and declared the doctrine of regeneration itself " an earthly thing " compared with the heavenly mysteries He had to tell,—those mysteries of His descent from heaven, sent by the Father to save the world. And therefore it is that in the midst of His ministry He opens this great discourse from which our text is taken, by declaring that the Son of Man has been " sealed," appointed and set apart, by the Father for the work of giving eternal life to men ; and when His disciples stumbled at the height of the great truth involved,—that He had come down from heaven to give His flesh as the food of the soul,—He sorrowfully added, " What, then, if you should see the Son of Man ascending where He was before ? "   And therefore it is that at the end of His life He compares His finished work with the joy a woman has after travail, when at length the child is born ; and declares that, having accomplished the work which the Father gave Him to do, the covenant condition is fulfilled, and the covenanted reward is at hand, and He is about to return to His primal glory. John's Gospel,—we ought not to miss it,—is the Gospel of the Covenant.

How our hearts should burn within us as we approach the last and most central question of all, and ask what is our Lord's account of the nature and terms of this mysterious but most blessed covenant, to fulfil the conditions of which He came down from heaven. We observe at once,—and with what emotions of gladness we ought to observe it,—that it concerns the salvation of men. And equally at once we observe, with still swelling emotion, that it is complete and perfect in its provisions,—that it provides for an entire and finished, for a sure and unfailing salvation. And we observe that this involves—as of course it must involve—the consequence that it is definite and precise in its terms,—that it contemplates definite and particularly designated men. " And this is the will of Him that sent Me, that of all that He hath given Me, I should lose nothing, but should raise it up at the last day." The will of the Father which Christ came down from heaven to do, concerned, then, distinctively : " all that He hath given Me." And His will with reference to these, which He sent the Son to perform, was not the making of some indefinite provision looking toward their rescue from sin and shame, but the definite actual, complete, and final saving of them : that " I should lose nothing of it, but should raise it up at the last day."

Let our hearts stand still while we read these great provisions. It is the testimony of the covenanted Son Himself, as to the terms of the covenant which He came to fulfil, that it had a definite and well-defined subject, and that it had a definite and fully-determined end,— not merely the rendering the salvation of men possible ; nor merely the removing of the legal obstacles in the way of the salvation of men ; nor merely the breaking down of whatever difficulties may stand in the path of the free outflow of God's love to men ; much less merely the introduction into the world of a better example of life than had hitherto been before men, or of a new divine force making for righteousness ; or the impressing of men with a deeper sense of the love of God for them, or of His hatred of sin ; but the actual, complete, and sure salvation of all that the Father had given the Son : " This is the will of Him that sent Me, that all that He hath given Me, I should lose nothing of it, but should raise it up at the last day."

In a word, we have presented to us here, in these

pregnant words, not only in outline, but in all its essential details, what has come to be known among us as the Covenant of Redemption. For what element of the doctrine is lacking here ? " I am come down from heaven, not to do My own will, but the will of Him that sent Me " : there is the assertion of an economic arrangement as the precondition of the incarnation, and of the prestipulation of the incarnated work. " And this is the will of Him that sent Me, that of all that He hath given Me I should lose nothing, but should raise it up at the last day " : there is the revelation of the contents of the pre-incarnation arrangement, and the provision through the incarnation for the certain salvation of a chosen body of lost men. " All that the Father giveth Me shall come unto Me " ; " No man can come unto Me except the Father which sent Me draw Him " : there is the twin definition of the subjects of the salvation. Or, if we desire further witness than this one passage, it is spread fully on the pages of this Gospel. Let us attend only to those calm and final words which, as His work was accomplishing, our blessed Redeemer addressed, not to us men, but to His Father, in a divinely assured assertion of His righteous claims upon the fruit of His work. " Father, the hour is come : glorify Thy Son, that the Son may glorify Thee : even as Thou gavest Him authority over all flesh, that to all that Thou hast given

Him, He should give to them eternal life. . . . I glorified Thee on the earth, having accomplished the work which Thou hast given Me to do. And now, O Father, glorify Thou Me with Thine own self, with the glory which I had with Thee before the world was. I manifested Thy name unto the men whom Thou didst give Me out of the world : Thine they were, and Thou didst give them to Me. . . . I pray for them ; I pray not for the world, but for those whom Thou hast given Me.'' All His work is in fulfilment of an arrangement with the Father ; and the whole of it, down to this High-Priestly prayer itself, making intercession for His own, concerns, primarily and in its chief import, those whom the Father gave Him out of the world, and secures beyond failure their complete salvation. This is the whole doctrine of the Covenant of Redemption : the Reformed theology has grasped it, and teaches it ; but it has not added one single thought to it.

And now let us bask a little, before we close, in the comforting assurances of this blessed teaching.

How the love of God is magnified to us by this teaching. It is not from a yesterday only that He has busied Himself with our salvation. In the depths of eternity our foreseen miseries were a cause of care to Him. In that mysterious intercourse between Father and Son, which is as eternal as the essence of Godhead itself, we—our state, our sin, our helplessness, and the dreadfulness of our condition and end,—were a subject of consideration and solicitude. What a God this is that is unveiled before us here. A God of holiness : a God so holy that even in the abyss of eternity-past He could not rest indifferent to the sin which was only after the lapse of innumerable ages to dawn in this corner of the as yet unexistent universe. A God of justice : a God so just that already His indignation burned against the as yet uncommitted sin of such petty creatures of His will as man. But a God of love : a love so inconceivably vast as already in the profundity of the unlimited past to brood over unimaginable plans of mercy toward these few guilty wretches among the numberless multitudes of His contemplated creatures. When the Psalmist raised his eyes to the heavens above, the work of the fingers of the Almighty, and considered the moon and stars which He had ordained, he was lost in a natural wonder that so great a Creator should concern Himself with so puny a creature : " What is man that Thou art mindful of him ? And the son of man that Thou shouldst visit him ? " But how much greater a marvel is before us now. It is not man as man,—a weak and puny creature—that we have to consider ; but man as sinner,—this weak and puny creature become vile and filthy, offensive and hateful to a holy and just God. It is not in contrast even with the grandeur of the worlds circling about worlds which crowd the depths of the heavens and dwarf the consequence of this speck of earth on the skirts of the universe which is our home, that we are to consider him ; but in contrast with the majesty of the increate Triune maker of all that is. It is not simply that God has taken notice of this sinful, puny creature, that we have to consider ; but that the All-Holy and All-Blessed God has felt care and solicitude for his fate and looked not at His own things in comparison with his. What indeed is sinful man that God should love him ; and before the foundations of the world should prepare to save him by so inconceivable a plan as to give His only-begotten Son as a ransom for his life ! My brethren, this is not to the glory of man, but to the glory of God ; it is not the expression of our dignity and worth, but raises our wondering hearts to the contemplation of the breadth and length, and height and depth of the love of God that passeth knowledge.

And how our appreciation of the perfection of the work of our Saviour is enhanced by this teaching. As it was upon no sudden caprice that He came into the world, but in execution of a long-cherished and thoroughly laid plan, so it was no partial work which He performed, but the whole work of salvation. " This is a faithful saying, and worthy of all acceptation, That Christ Jesus came into the world to *save* sinners." And this He has accomplished, even to the uttermost. When He cried upon the cross, as His agony went out in the darkness of death,—a death for us—in those words of deepest import and of mighty power, " It is finished ! " —when in His great sacerdotal prayer, he proleptically declared that He had " accomplished the work " which the Father " had given Him to do," and was now ready to lay aside His humiliation and re-enter His glory : the precise thing which He published as " finished " and " accomplished " was salvation. All has been done by Him. His saving work neither needs nor admits of supplementary addition by any needy child of man, even to the extent of an iota. When we look to Him we are raising grateful eyes, not to one who invites us to save ourselves ; nor merely to one who has broken out a path, in which walking, we may attain to salvation ; nor yet merely to one who offers us a salvation wrought out by Him, on a condition ; but to one who has *saved* us,—who is at once the beginning and the middle and the end of our salvation, the author and the finisher of our faith.

What can we possibly need that we do not find provided in Him ? Do we hopelessly groan under the curse of the broken law, hanging menacingly over us ? Christ has " redeemed us from the curse of the law, having been made a curse for us." Do we know that only he that worketh righteousness is acceptable to

God, and despair of attaining life on so unachievable a condition ? Christ Jesus "hath of God been made unto us righteousness." Do we loathe ourselves in the pollution of our sins, and know that God is greater than we, and that we must be an offence in His holy sight ? The blood of Christ cleanseth us from all sin. But do we not need faith, that we may be made one with Him and so secure those benefits ? Faith, too, is the gift of God : and that we believe on Him is granted by God in the behalf of Christ. Have we sought to run, and learned by bitter experience that it is not of him that runneth nor of him that willeth ? We may learn too by a happy experience that it is of God that showeth mercy and that worketh in us both the willing and the doing. Nothing has been forgotten, nothing neglected, nothing left unprovided. In the person of Jesus Christ, the great God, in His perfect wisdom and unfailing power, has taken our place before the outraged justice of God and under His perfect law, and has wrought out a complete salvation.

What an indefectible certitude of salvation is given by this great teaching. If Christ Jesus came to save and has saved, how can salvation fail ? If the free gift of God is eternal life in Christ Jesus our Lord, how can this eternal life thus freely given go out in time, and fail to accord with its very designation as eternal ? If Christ has undertaken not merely to open a way of salvation to us, but to save us ; if He came into the world for the precise purpose of performing *this* will of God, " that of all that He hath given Him, He should lose nothing, but should raise it up at the last day,"—what possibility lies open of the failure of this great design, framed in eternity by Triune Godhead, and executed in time by none other than the strong Son of God ? Therefore our gracious Lord assures us : " All that the Father giveth Me *shall come unto Me,* and him that cometh unto Me I will in no wise cast out." And therefore His servant, condescending to the weakness of our fears, argues with us : " God commendeth His love towards us, in that, while we were yet sinners, Christ died for us. Much more, then, being justified by His blood, shall we be saved from wrath by Him." Oh, the certitude in that " much more." " If God be for us," he argues again, " who can be against us ? He that spared not His own Son, but delivered Him up for us all, how shall He not also with Him freely give us all things ? . . . Who shall separate us from the love of Christ ? " O weak and trembling soul, can you not find, not courage merely, but certitude in this ? What matters your weakness ? Your salvation rests not on it, but on God's strength. He loves you ; He determined to save you ; He sent His Son to save you ; He has come to do it : He has done it. You are saved : it cannot fail, unless God's set purpose can fail ; unless Christ's power to save can fail ; unless His promises of love can fail.

What a clear ground of assurance of salvation is furnished by this great teaching. Does some wayward spirit say : " All this is true only of the elect, those whom the Father gave to Christ. And I, alas ! how may I know that I am of the elect ? " Ah, self-tormenting soul, why expend strength in prying into God's secrets, instead of taking Him at His word ? It is true indeed that it is only those whom He has given to Christ that Christ has saved ; and the comfort, as the salvation, is for them alone. But it is not true that God requires election of you for salvation, or offers predestination to you as the way of life. He offers you not predestination, but Christ ; and He requires of you not election, but faith. Do you make election itself a ground of doubt and despair ? This, says an old Puritan, is indeed to gather poison out of the sweetest of herbs. " God layeth it as a duty upon every one to repent and believe, to come to Him and he shall have rest to his soul. . . . If, then, thou believest, thou repentest, this may be a sure testimony unto thee of thy everlasting glory."

Election does indeed lie at the root of our salvation : but faith is the proof of election. Are we saved ? The question is resolved in this : Do we believe in Jesus

Christ ? Christ indeed says, " This is the will of Him who sent Me, that of *all that He hath given Me*, I should lose nothing, but should raise it up at the last day." Here is election the root of the saving work of Christ. But have you failed to note or to remember that He immediately adds : " For this is the will of My Father, that *every one that beholdeth the Son and believeth on Him* should have eternal life, and that I should raise him up at the last day." Here is the work of Christ received in faith the ground of salvation : and here is faith laying hold of Christ the evidence of salvation. And therefore it is not only said, " All that the Father giveth Me shall come unto Me," but it is immediately added : " *And him that cometh to Me I will in no wise cast out.*" These words are gracious enough in their broadest sense to send a thrill of joy through the heart. But there lies hidden within them a further delicate grace which is lost in the English translation. The word for " come " is so varied in the two clauses as to lay the stress in the first instance " upon the successful issue of the coming, the arrival," and in the second " on the process of the coming and the welcome." " All that the Father giveth Me shall come unto Me "—shall certainly and unfailingly reach Me. " And him that cometh unto Me I will in no wise cast out "—" him that is in the process of coming,"—yea, even though he is but just begun, with weak and faltering steps, even such an one as this who is but beginning to come—" I will in no wise cast out."

What a blessed assurance, when faith is made thus not the ground of salvation, not the condition of salvation, but its evidence ! It is here that the sweet herb of election begins to pour forth its refreshing cordial. Men may tell us, indeed, " Believe and you shall be saved," while still making faith the ground or the condition of salvation. And, then, with what dreadful solicitude will we pluck up our faith over and over again by the roots, to examine it with anxious fear. Is it the right faith ? Is it a strong enough faith ? Do I believe aright ? Do I believe enough ? Shall I abide in my belief until the end ? Dreadful uncertainty ! Inexpressible misery of ineradicable doubt ! It is only when we have learned from such words of our Master as those before us to-day, that we dare say to our souls not only, Believe and ye shall be saved ! but those other words of deeper meaning and fuller comfort, caught from the Master's own blessed lips : Believe and ye *are* saved ! " Verily, verily, I say unto you," says our Saviour in words which sum up previous teachings, " He that heareth My words and believeth Him that sent Me, *hath* eternal life, and cometh not into judgment, but *hath* passed out of death into life." Blessed John, who so caught his Master's words and recorded them for us. When faith is thus made not the ground or the condition, but the evidence of salvation, our eternal bliss is no longer suspended in any sense on aught that we are or do, but hangs solely on the work of Christ, doing His Father's will. Faith, even faith, as the ground or condition of salvation, may be also the ground of despair : but faith as the proof of salvation is the charter of assured though humble hope. It takes hold of the " strong Son of God, immortal love," and of the indefectible purpose of Almighty grace which cannot fail or know any shadow of turning. This we owe to that doctrine of the eternal covenant which our blessed Saviour reveals to us in the words on which we have meditated to-day. Because of its blessed provisions we can cry joy to our souls, though they tremble with natural fear and can scarce believe that Christ will save such faithless souls as they. Though they have faith but as a grain of mustard-seed, they *are* saved already. For, this is the will of Him who sent our Redeemer, that of all that He gave Him He should lose nothing, but should raise it up at the last day : for this is the will of the Father, that every one that beholdeth the Son and believeth on Him should have eternal life and He should raise him up at the last day.

Beloved, do not, I beseech you, ground your salvation even in your faith. Ground it only in Jesus Christ who alone is your Saviour. And remember this,—that it is not your faith that saves you but

God, and God alone, by whom it is that faith is wrought in your soul, and by whose power it is that you are guarded through your faith unto that salvation which is reserved for you in heaven, and which shall without fail be revealed at the last day. Can your faith fail ? Nay, forget your faith. Certainly the power of God, your Almighty Saviour, through which alone you have faith and which is pledged to your guarding, cannot fail !

IMITATING THE INCARNATION

PHILIPPIANS ii. 5–8 :—Let this mind be in you, which was also in Christ Jesus : who, being in the form of God, thought it not robbery to be equal with God : but made Himself of no reputation, and took upon Him the form of a servant, and was made in the likeness of men : and being found in fashion as a man, He humbled Himself, and became obedient unto death, even the death of the cross.

IMITATING THE INCARNATION

"CHRIST our Example." After "Christ our Redeemer," no words can more deeply stir the Christian heart than these. Every Christian joyfully recognizes the example of Christ, as, in the admirable words of a great Scotch commentator, a body " of living legislation," as " law, embodied and pictured in a perfect humanity." In Him, in a word, we find the moral ideal historically realized, and we bow before it as sublime and yearn after it with all the assembled desires of our renewed souls.

How lovingly we follow in thought every footstep of the Son of Man, on the rim of hills that shut in the emerald cup of Nazareth, on the blue marge of Gennesaret, over the mountains of Judea, and long to walk in spirit by His side. He came to save every age, says Irenæus, and therefore He came as an infant, a child, a boy, a youth, and a man. And there is no age that cannot find its example in Him. We see Him, the properest child that ever was given to a mother's arms, through all the years of childhood at Nazareth " subjecting Himself to His parents." We see Him a youth, labouring day by day contentedly at His father's bench, in this lower sphere, too, with no other thought than to be " about His father's business." We see Him in

His holy manhood, going, " as His custom was,"
Sabbath by Sabbath, to the synagogue,—God as He
was, not too good to worship with His weaker brethren.
And then the horizon broadens. We see Him at the
banks of Jordan, because it became Him to fulfil every
righteousness, meekly receiving the baptism of repentance for us. We see Him in the wilderness, calmly
rejecting the subtlest trials of the evil one : refusing
to supply His needs by a misuse of His divine power,
repelling the confusion of tempting God with trusting
God, declining to seek His Father's ends by any other
than His Father's means. We see Him among the
thousands of Galilee, anointed of God with the Holy
Ghost and power, going about doing good : with no
pride of birth, though He was a king ; with no pride
of intellect, though omniscience dwelt within Him ;
with no pride of power, though all power in heaven
and earth was in His hands ; or of station, though the
fulness of the Godhead dwelt in Him bodily ; or of
superior goodness or holiness : but in lowliness of
mind esteeming every one better than Himself, healing
the sick, casting out devils, feeding the hungry, and
everywhere breaking to men the bread of life. We see
Him everywhere offering to men His life for the salvation of their souls : and when, at last, the forces of
evil gathered thick around Him, walking, alike without
display and without dismay, the path of suffering

appointed for Him, and giving His life at Calvary that through His death the world might live.

" Which of you convinceth Me of sin ? " is too low a question. Who can find in all His life a single lack, a single failure to set us a perfect example ? In what difficulty of life, in what trial, in what danger or uncertainty, when we turn our eyes to Him, do we fail to find just the example that we need ? And if perchance we are, by the grace of God, enabled to walk with Him but a step in the way, how our hearts burn within us with longing to be always with Him,—to be strengthened by the almighty power of God in the inner man, to make every footprint which He has left in the world a stepping-stone to climb upward over His divine path. Do we not rightly say that next to our longing to be in Christ is our corresponding longing to be like Christ ; that only second in our hearts to His great act of obedience unto death by which He became our Saviour, stands His holy life in our world of sin, by which He becomes our example ?

Of course our text is not singular in calling upon us to make Christ our example. " Be ye imitators of me, even as I also am of Christ Jesus," is rather the whole burden of the ethical side of Paul's teaching. And in this, too, he was but the imitator of his Lord, who pleads with us to " learn of Him because He is meek and lowly in heart." The peculiarity of our present passage is only that it takes us back of Christ's earthly life and bids us imitate Him in the great act of His incarnation itself. Not, of course, as if the implication were that we were equal with Christ and needed to stoop to such service as He performed. " Why art thou proud, O man ? " Augustine asks pointedly. " God for thee became low. Thou wouldst perhaps be ashamed to initate a lowly man ; then at least imitate the lowly God. The Son of God came in the character of man and was made low. . . . He, since He was God, became man : do thou, O man, recognize that thou art man. Thy entire humility is to know thyself." The very force of the appeal lies, in a word, in the infinite exaltation of Christ above us : and the mention of the incarnation is the apostle's reminder to us of the ineffable majesty which was by nature His to whom he would raise our admiring eyes. Paul prises at our hearts here with the great lever of the deity of our exemplar. He calls upon us to do nothing less than to be imitators of God. " What encouragement is greater than this ? " cries Chrysostom, with his instinctive perception of the motive-springs of the human heart. " Nothing arouses a great soul to the performance of good works so much as learning that in this it is likened to God." And here, too, Paul is but the follower of his Lord : " Be ye merciful, as your Father which is in heaven is merciful," are words which fell from His divine lips, altogether similar in their implication to Paul's words in the text : " Let it be this mind that is in you, which also was in Christ Jesus." It is the spirit which animated our Lord in the act of His incarnation which His apostle would see us imitate. He would have us in all our acts to be like Christ, as He showed Himself to be in the innermost core of His being, when He became poor, He that was rich, that we by His poverty might be made rich.

We perceive, then, that the exhortation of the apostle gathers force for itself from the deity of Christ, and from the nature of the transaction by which He, being God, was brought into this sphere of dependent, earthly life in which we live by nature. It is altogether natural, then, that he sharpens his appeal by reminding his readers somewhat fully who Christ was and what He did for our salvation, in order that, having the facts more vividly before their minds, they may more acutely feel the spirit by which He was animated. Thus, in a perfectly natural way, Paul is led, not to inform his readers but to remind them, in a few quick and lively phrases which do not interrupt the main lines of discourse but rather etch them in with a deeper colour, of what we may call the whole doctrine of the Person of Christ. With such a masterly hand, or let us rather say with such an eager spirit and such a loving clearness and firmness of touch, has he done this, that these few purely incidental words constitute one of the most complete statements of an essential doctrine to be found within the whole compass of the Scriptures. Though compressed within the limits of three short verses, it ranks in fulness of exposition with the already marvellously concise out-line of the same doctrine given in the opening verses of the Gospel of John. Whenever the subtleties of heresy confuse our minds as we face the problems which have been raised about the Person of our Lord, it is pre-eminently to these verses that we flee to have our apprehension purified, and our thinking corrected. The sharp phrases cut their way through every error : or, as we may better say, they are like a flight of swift arrows, each winged to the joints of the harness.

The golden-mouthed preacher of the ancient Church, impressed with this fulness of teaching and inspired himself to one of his loftiest flights by the verve of the apostle's crisp language, pictures the passage itself as an arena, and the Truth, as it runs burning through the clauses, as the victorious chariot dashing against and overthrowing its contestants one after the other, until at last, amid the clamour of applause which rises from every side to heaven, it springs alone towards the goal, with coursers winged with joy sweeping like a single flash over the ground. One by one he points out the heresies concerning the Person of Christ which had

sprung up in the ancient Church, as clause by clause the
text smites and destroys them ; and is not content
until he shows how the knees of all half-truths and
whole falsehoods alike concerning this great matter are
made by these searching words to bow before our
Saviour's perfect deity, His complete humanity, and
the unity of His person. The magic of the passage has
lost none of its virtue with the millennium and a half
which has fled by since John Chrysostom electrified
Constantinople with his golden words : this sword of
the Spirit is as keen to-day as it was then, and happy
is the man who knows its temper and has the arm to
wield it. But we must not lose ourselves in a purely
theological interest with such a passage before us.
Rather let us keep our eyes, for this hour, on Paul's
main purpose, and seek to feel the force of the example
of Christ as he here advances it, for the government of
our lives. But to do this, as he points it with so full a
reference to the Person of Christ, following him we must
begin by striving to realize who and what our Lord
was, who set us this example.

Let us observe, then, first, that the actor to whose
example Paul would direct our eyes, is declared by him
to have been no other than God Himself. " Who was
before in the form of God," are his words : and they are
words than which no others could be chosen which
would more explicitly or with more directness assert

the deity of the person who is here designated by the name of Christ Jesus. After the wear and tear of two thousand years on the phrases, it would not be surprising if we should fail to feel this as strongly as we ought. Let us remember that the phraseology which Paul here employs was the popular usage of his day, though first given general vogue by the Aristotelian philosophy : and that it was accordingly the most natural language for strongly asserting the deity of Christ which could suggest itself to him. As you know, this mode of speech resolved everything into its matter and its form, —into the bare material out of which it is made, and that body of characterizing qualities which constitute it what it is. " Form," in a word, is equivalent to our phrase " specific character." If we may illustrate great things by small, we may say, in this manner of speech, that the " matter " of a sword, for instance, is steel, while its " form " is that whole body of characterizing qualities which distinguish a sword from all other pieces of steel, and which, therefore, make this particular piece of steel distinctively a sword. In this case, these are, of course, largely matters of shape and contour. But now the steel itself, which constitutes the matter of the sword, has also its " matter " and its " form " : its " matter " being metal, and its " form " being the whole body of qualities that distinguish steel from other metals, and make this metal steel. Going back

still a step, metal itself has its " matter " and " form " ;
its " matter " being material substance and its " form "
that body of qualities which distinguish metallic from
other kinds of substance. And last of all, matter itself
has its " matter," namely, substance, and its " form,"
namely, the qualities which distinguish material
from spiritual substance, and make this substance
what we call matter. The same mode of speech is,
of course, equally applicable to the spiritual sphere.
The " matter " of the human spirit is bare spiritual
substance, while its " form " is that body of qualities
which constitute this spirit a human spirit, and in
the absence of which, or by the change of which, this
spirit would cease to be human and become some
other kind of spirit. The " matter " of an angel, again,
is bare spiritual substance, while the " form " is the
body of qualities which make this spirit specifically an
angel. So, too, with God : the " matter " of God is
bare spiritual substance, and the " form " is that body
of qualities which distinguish Him from all other
spiritual beings, which constitute Him God, and without which He would not be God. What Paul asserts
then, when he says that Christ Jesus existed in the
" form of God," is that He had all those characterizing
qualities which make God God, the presence of which
constitutes God, and in the absence of which God does
not exist. He who is " in the form of God," is God.

Nor is it without significance that, out of the possible modes of expression open to him, Paul was led to choose just this mode of asserting the deity of our Lord. His mind in this passage was not on the bare divine essence ; it was upon the divine qualities and prerogatives of Christ. It is not the abstract conception that Christ is God that moves us to our deepest admiration for His sublime act of self-sacrifice : but rather our concrete realization that He was all that God is, and had all that God has,—that God's omnipotence was His, His infinite exaltation, His unapproachable blessedness. Therefore Paul is instinctively led to choose an expression which tells us not the bare fact that Christ was God, but that He was " in the form of God,"—that He had in full possession all those characterizing qualities which, taken together, make God that all-holy, perfect, all-blessed being which we call God. Thus the apostle prepares his readers for the great example by quickening their apprehension not only of who, but of what Christ was.

Let us note, then, secondly, that the apostle outlines for us very fully the action which this divine being performed. " He took the form of a servant by coming into the likeness of men ; and being found in fashion as a man, He humbled Himself by becoming subject even unto death, and that the death of the cross." There is no metamorphosis of substance asserted here : the " form of God " is not said to have been transmuted into the " form of a servant " ; but He who was " in the form of God " is declared to have taken also to Himself " the form of a servant." Nor is there, on the other hand, any deceptive show of an unreal humiliation brought before us here : He took, not the appearance, mere state and circumstances, or mere work and performance, but veritably " the form of a servant,"—all those essential qualities and attributes which belong to, and constitute a being " a servant." The assumption involved the taking of an actually servile nature, as well as of a sub-ordinate station and a servant's work. And therefore it is at once further explained in both its mode and its effects. He took the form of a servant " by coming into the likeness of men " : He did not become merely a man, but by taking the form of a servant He came into a state in which He appeared as man. His humanity was real and complete : but it was not all, —He remained God in assuming humanity, and there-fore only appeared as man, not became only man. And by taking the form of a servant and thus being found in fashion as a man, He became subject to obedi-ence,—an obedience pressed so far in its humiliation that it extended even unto death, and that the shameful death of the cross. Words cannot adequately paint the depth of this humiliation. But this it was,—the taking of the form of a servant with its resultant necessity of obedience to such a bitter end,—this it was that He who was by nature in the form of God,— in the full possession and use of all the divine attributes and qualities, powers and prerogatives,—was willing to do for us.

Let us observe, then, thirdly, that the apostle clearly announces to us the spirit in which our Lord performed this great act. "Although He was in the form of God, He yet did not consider His being on an equality with God a precious prize to be eagerly retained, but made no account of Himself, taking the form of a servant." It was then in a spirit of pure unselfishness and self-sacrifice, that looked not on its own things but on the things of others, that under the force of love esteemed others more than Himself,—it was in this mind : or, in the apostle's own words, it was as not considering His essential equality with God as a precious possession, but making no account of Himself,—it was in this mind, that Christ Jesus who was before in the form of God took the form of a servant. This was the state of mind that led Him to so marvellous an act,— no compulsion from His Father, no desires for Himself, no hope of gain or fear of loss, but simple, unselfish, self-sacrificing love.

Now it is not to be overlooked that some of the clauses the meaning of which we have sought to fathom,

are differently explained among expositors. Nevertheless, although I have sought to adduce them so as to
bring out the apostle's exact meaning, and although I
believe that his appeal acquires an additional point and
a stronger leverage when they are thus understood, it
remains true that the main drift of the passage is un-
affected by any of the special interpretations which
reasonable expositors have put upon the several clauses.
These divergent expositions do seriously affect our
doctrine of the Person of Christ.   In particular, all the
forms of the popular modern doctrine of *kenosis* or
exinanition, which teaches that the divine Logos in
becoming man " emptied Himself," and thus, that the
very God in a more or less literal sense contracted
Himself to the limits of humanity, find their chief,
almost their sole Biblical basis in what appears to me a
gratuitously erroneous interpretation of one of these
clauses,—that one which the Authorized Version
renders, " He made Himself of no reputation," and
which I have ventured to render, " He made no
account of Himself," that is, in comparison with the
needs of others ; but which the theologians in question, followed, unfortunately as I think, by the Revised
Version, render with an excessive literality, " He
emptied Himself," thereby resurrecting the literal
physical sense of the word in an unnatural context.
We have many reasons to give why this is an illegiti-

mate rendering ; chief among which are, that the word
is commonly employed in its figurative sense and that
the intrusion of the literal sense here is forbidden by
the context. But it is unnecessary to pause to argue
the point. Whatever the conclusion might be, the
main drift of the passage remains the same. No interpretation of this phrase can destroy the outstanding
fact that the passage at large places before our wondering eyes the two *termini* of " the form of God " and
" the form of a servant," involving obedience even unto
a shameful death ; and " measures the extent of our
Lord's self-denying grace by the distance between
equality with God and a public execution on a gibbet."
In any case the emphasis of the passage is thrown upon
the spirit of self-sacrificing unselfishness as the impelling
cause of Christ's humiliation, which the apostle adduces
here in order that the sight of it may impel us also to
take no account of ourselves, but to estimate lightly all
that we are or have in comparison with the claims of
others on our love and devotion. The one subject of
the whole passage is Christ's marvellous self-sacrifice.
Its one exhortation is, " Let it be this mind that is also
in you." As we read through the passage we may, by
contact with the full mind and heart of the apostle,
learn much more than this. But let us not fail to grasp
this, his chief message to us here,—that Christ Jesus,
though He was God, yet cared less for His equality with

God, cared less for Himself and His own things, than He did for us, and therefore gave Himself for us.

Firmly grasping this, then, as the essential content and special message of the passage, there are some inferences that flow from it which we cannot afford not to remind ourselves of.

And first of these is a very great and marvellous one,—that we have a God who is capable of self-sacrifice for us. It was although He was in the form of God, that Christ Jesus did not consider His being on an equality with God so precious a possession that He could not lay it aside, but rather made no account of Himself. It was our God who so loved us that He gave Himself for us. Now, herein is a wonderful thing. Men tell us that God is, by the very necessity of His nature, incapable of passion, incapable of being moved by inducements from without ; that He dwells in holy calm and unchangeable blessedness, untouched by human sufferings or human sorrows for ever,—haunting

> The lucid interspace of world and world,
> Where never creeps a cloud, nor moves a wind,
> Nor ever falls the least white star of snow,
> Nor ever lowest roll of thunder moans,
> Nor sound of human sorrow mounts to mar
> His sacred, everlasting calm.

Let us bless our God that it is not true. God can feel ; God does love. We have Scriptural warrant for believing, as it has been perhaps somewhat inadequately but not misleadingly phrased, that moral heroism has a place within the sphere of the divine nature : we have Scriptural warrant for believing that, like the old hero of Zurich, God has reached out loving arms and gathered into His own bosom that forest of spears which otherwise had pierced ours.

But is not this gross anthropomorphism ? We are careless of names : it is the truth of God. And we decline to yield up the God of the Bible and the God of our hearts to any philosophical abstraction. We have and we must have an ethical God ; a God whom we can love, and in whom we can trust. We may feel awe in the presence of the Absolute, as we feel awe in the presence of the storm or of the earthquake : we may feel our dependence in its presence, as we feel our help-lessness before the tornado or the flood. But we cannot love it ; we cannot trust it ; and our hearts, which are just as trustworthy a guide as our dialectics, cry out for a God whom we may love and trust. We decline once for all to subject our whole conception of God to the category of the Absolute, which, as has been truly said, " like Pharaoh's lean kine, devours all other attri-butes." Neither is this an unphilosophical procedure. As has been set forth renewedly by Andrew Seth, " we should be unfaithful to the fundamental principle of the theory of knowledge " " if we did not interpret by means of the highest category within our reach."

" We should be false to ourselves, if we denied in God what we recognize as the source of dignity and worth in ourselves." In order to escape an anthropomorphic God, we must not throw ourselves at the feet of a zoomorphic or an amorphic one.

Nevertheless, let us rejoice that our God has not left us by searching to find Him out. Let us rejoice that He has plainly revealed Himself to us in His Word as a God who loves us, and who, because He loves us, has sacrificed Himself for us. Let us remember that it is a fundamental conception in the Christian idea of God that God is love ; and that it is the fundamental dogma of the Christian religion that God so loved us that He gave Himself for us. Accordingly, the primary presupposition of our present passage is that our God was capable of, and did actually perform, this amazing act of unselfish self-sacrifice for the good of man.

The second inference that we should draw from our passage consists simply in following the apostle in his application of this divine example to our human life : a life of self-sacrificing unselfishness is the most divinely beautiful life that man can lead. He whom as our Master we have engaged to obey, whom as our Example we are pledged to imitate, is presented to us here as the great model of self-sacrificing unselfishness. " Let this mind be in you, which was also in Christ Jesus," is the apostle's pleading. We need to note carefully, however, that it is not self-depreciation, but self-abnegation, that is thus commended to us. If we would follow Christ, we must, every one of us, not in pride but in humility, yet not in lowness but in lowliness, not degrade ourselves but forget ourselves, and seek every man not his own things but those of others.

Who does not see that in this organism which we call human society, such a mode of life is the condition of all real help and health ? There is, no doubt, another ideal of life far more grateful to our fallen human nature, an ideal based on arrogance, assumption, self-assertion, working through strife, and issuing in conquest,—conquest of a place for ourselves, a position, the admiration of man, power over men. We see its working on every side of us : in the competition of business life,—in the struggle for wealth on the one side, forcing a struggle for bare bread on the other ; in social life,—in the fierce battle of men and women for leading parts in the farce of social display ; even in the Church itself, and among the Churches, where, too, unhappily, arrogant pretension and unchristian self-assertion do not fail to find their temporal reward. But it is clear that this is not Christ's ideal, nor is it to this that He has set us His perfect example. " He made no account of Himself " : though He was in the form of God, He yet looked not upon His equality with God as a possession to be prized when He could by forgetting self rescue those whom He was not ashamed, amid all His glory, to call His brethren.

Are there any whom you and I are ashamed to call our brethren ?   O that the divine ideal of life as service could take possession of our souls !   O that we could remember at all times and in all relations that the Son of Man came into the world to minister, and by His ministry has glorified all ministering for ever. O that we could once for all grasp the meaning of the great fact that self-forgetfulness and self-sacrifice express the divine ideals of life.

And thus we are led to a third inference, which comes to us from the text : that it is difficult to set a limit to the self-sacrifice which the example of Christ calls upon us to be ready to undergo for the good of our brethren.   It is comparatively easy to recognize that the ideal of the Christian life is self-sacrificing unselfishness, and to allow that it is required of those who seek to enter into it, to subordinate self and to seek first the kingdom of God.   But is it so easy to acknowledge, even to ourselves, that this is to be read not generally merely but in detail, and is to be applied not only to some eminent saints but to all who would be Christ's servants ?—that it is required of us, and that what is required of us is not some self-denial but all self-sacrifice ?   Yet is it not to this that the example of Christ would lead us ?—not, of course, to self-degradation, not to self-effacement exactly, but to complete self-abnegation, entire and ungrudging self-sacrifice ? Is it to be unto death itself ? Christ died. Are we to endure wrongs ? What wrongs did He not meekly bear ? Are we to surrender our clear and recognized rights ? Did Christ stand upon His unquestioned right of retaining His equality with God ? Are we to endure unnatural evils, permit ourselves to be driven into inappropriate situations, unresistingly sustain injurious and unjust imputations and attacks ? What more unnatural than that the God of the universe should become a servant in the world, ministering not to His Father only, but also to His creatures,—our Lord and Master washing our very feet ? What more abhorrent than that God should die ? There is no length to which Christ's self-sacrifice did not lead Him. These words are dull and inexpressive ; we cannot enter into thoughts so high. He who was in the form of God took such thought for us, that He made no account of Himself. Into the immeasurable calm of the divine blessedness He permitted this thought to enter, " I will die for men ! " And so mighty was His love, so colossal the divine purpose to save, that He thought nothing of His divine majesty, nothing of His unsullied blessedness, nothing of His equality with God, but, absorbed in us,—our needs, our misery, our helplessness—He made no account of Himself.

If this is to be our example, what limit can we set to our self-sacrifice ? Let us remember that we are no longer our own but Christ's, bought with the price of His precious blood, and are henceforth to live, not for ourselves but for Him,—for Him in His creatures, serving Him in serving them. Let all thought of our dignity, our possessions, our rights, perish out of sight, when Christ's service calls to us. Let the mind be in us that was also in Him, when He took no account of Himself, but, God as He was, took the form of a servant and humbled Himself,—He who was Lord,—to lowly obedience even unto death, and that the death of the cross. In such a mind as this, where is the end of unselfishness ?

Let us not, however, do the apostle the injustice of fancying that this is a morbid life to which he summons us. The self-sacrifice to which he exhorts us, unlimited as it is, going all lengths and starting back blanched at nothing, is nevertheless not an unnatural life. After all, it issues not in the destruction of self, but only in the destruction of selfishness ; it leads us not to a Buddha-like unselfing, but to a Christ-like self-development. It would not make us into

> deedless dreamers lazying out a life
> Of self-suppression, not of selfless love,

but would light the flames of a love within us by which we would literally " ache for souls." The example of

Christ and the exhortation of Paul found themselves upon a sense of the unspeakable value of souls. Our Lord took no account of Himself, only because the value of the souls of men pressed upon His heart. And following Him, we are not to consider our own things, but those of others, just because everything earthly that concerns us is as nothing compared with their eternal welfare.

Our self-abnegation is thus not for our own sake, but for the sake of others. And thus it is not to mere self-denial that Christ calls us, but specifically to self-sacrifice : not to unselfing ourselves, but to unselfishing ourselves. Self-denial for its own sake is in its very nature ascetic, monkish. It concentrates our whole attention on self—self-knowledge, self-control—and can therefore eventuate in nothing other than the very apotheosis of selfishness. At best it succeeds only in subjecting the outer self to the inner self, or the lower self to the higher self ; and only the more surely falls into the slough of self-seeking, that it partially conceals the selfishness of its goal by refining its ideal of self and excluding its grosser and more outward elements. Self-denial, then, drives to the cloister ; narrows and contracts the soul ; murders within us all innocent desires, dries up all the springs of sympathy, and nurses and coddles our self-importance until we grow so great in our own esteem as to be careless of the trials and sufferings, the joys and aspirations, the strivings and failures and successes of our fellow-men. Self-denial, thus understood, will make us cold, hard, unsympathetic,—proud, arrogant, self-esteeming,—fanatical, overbearing, cruel. It may make monks and Stoics,— it cannot make Christians.

It is not to this that Christ's example calls us. He did not cultivate self, even His divine self : He took no account of self. He was not led by His divine impulse out of the world, driven back into the recesses of His own soul to brood morbidly over His own needs, until to gain His own seemed worth all sacrifice to Him. He was led by His love for others into the world, to forget Himself in the needs of others, to sacrifice self once for all upon the altar of sympathy. Self-sacrifice brought Christ into the world. And self-sacrifice will lead us, His followers, not away from but into the midst of men. Wherever men suffer, there will we be to comfort. Wherever men strive, there will we be to help. Wherever men fail, there will be we to uplift. Wherever men succeed, there will we be to rejoice. Self-sacrifice means not indifference to our times and our fellows : it means absorption in them. It means forgetfulness of self in others. It means entering into every man's hopes and fears, longings and despairs : it means manysidedness of spirit, multiform activity, multiplicity of sympathies. It means richness of development. It means not that we should live one life, but a thousand lives,—binding ourselves to a thousand souls by the filaments of so loving a sympathy that their lives become ours. It means that all the experiences of men shall smite our souls and shall beat and batter these stubborn hearts of ours into fitness for their heavenly home. It is, after all, then, the path to the highest possible development, by which alone we can be made truly men.

Not that we shall undertake it with this end in view. This were to dry up its springs at their source. We cannot be self-consciously self-forgetful, selfishly unselfish. Only, when we humbly walk this path, seeking truly in it not our own things but those of others, we shall find the promise true, that he who loses his life shall find it. Only, when, like Christ, and in loving obedience to His call and example, we take no account of ourselves, but freely give ourselves to others, we shall find, each in his measure, the saying true of himself also : " Wherefore also God hath highly exalted him." The path of self-sacrifice is the path to glory.

WILLIAM BRENDON AND SON, LTD., PRINTERS, PLYMOUTH